THE SENSUOUS WOMAN

The

Sensuous

Woman

by J.

The first *how-to* book for the female who
yearns to be *all* woman

CASTLE BOOKS, INC.

To
L.F., J.N., O.B.S., A.V.N., and A.V.E.
who made learning such a pleasure

Arrangement has been made to publish this edition by Castle Bo
a division of Book Sales Inc. of Secaucus, New Jersey

ISBN No.: 0-89009-489-6

August—1981

Manufactured in the United States of America

Contents

CONTENTS

CONTENTS

CONTENTS

In the Beginning . . .

For the last five years men have been telling me the most delicious things—that I'm sexy, all woman, that perfect combination of a lady in the living room and a marvelous bitch in bed, sensual, beautiful, a modern Aphrodite, maddeningly exciting, the epitome of the Sensuous Woman.

Some of the most interesting men in America have fallen in love with me. I have received marriage proposals from such diverse personalities as a concert pianist, a best-selling author, the producer of three of America's most popular television shows, a bomb expert for the CIA, a trial attorney, an apple grower, a TV and radio star and a tax expert.

Yet you'd never believe it if we came face to face on the street, for I'm not particularly pretty. I have heavy thighs, lumpy hips, protruding teeth, a ski jump nose, poor posture, flat feet and uneven ears.

I never wear tight skirts, low-cut dresses or bikinis.

I am not brilliant and I don't have a magnetic personality. In fact, I'm shy.

Mothers, wives and girl friends think of me as the wholesome, apple pie, girl-next-door type (which, translated, means non-sexy).

But while those mothers, wives and girl friends are burning up over that spectacular-looking blonde undulating provocatively in the peekaboo leopard print, I'm the one that's having the wonderful time—and getting and *keeping* men.

For, through intelligence and hard work, I have become a Sensuous Woman.

And that's what almost every man wants.

More than beauty

More than brilliance

More than great housekeeping abilities

More than a model mother to his children

He wants a Sensuous Woman

Because she makes him *know* that he is the most remarkable man that ever lived.

Women who can clean, look good and mother children are a dollar a dozen, but a woman who can make a man feel his uniqueness is worth the world to him.

Even if you are knock-kneed, flat-chested, cross-eyed and balding, you can learn to make him feel that way and, in doing so, reap wonderful benefits for yourself, such as *the enriching experience of a really joyous and fulfilling sex life*. To discover the how-tos of all the erotic pleasures that await you, turn the page and start reading.

1.

Sex—Why It's Even Ahead of Horse Racing as the Nation's Number One Sport

Some of the most confusing, disappointing and lonely experiences of my life have been sexual.

Some of the most piercingly beautiful, earthshaking and companionable experiences of my life have also been sexual.

Having gone through both good and bad, I prefer good.

So will you.

Sex is an inescapable part of us. It is there

from the moment of birth when we are given a sexual identity—boy or girl—and it is with us until the day we die—when it goes on the death certificate.

You're not going to be able to skip out on sex, so accept it and look toward the good. Those of us who have been labeled female owe it to ourselves to reap the considerable benefits, such as—well, how about these for openers?—the right to be soft and fragile; the luxury of having doors opened, packages carried, cigarettes lighted, chairs pulled out for us; the pleasure of being able to cry openly when we feel like it; the joy of giving everything of ourselves to the men we love; and (sometimes) the delight of receiving great loot like diamond necklaces, ruby bracelets and mink coats.

You can also consider yourself lucky to have been born after 1900, for you have entered a world that has radically changed, thanks to the delightfully shocking discovery that women, *nice women,* are, given the chance, able to enjoy themselves in bed and are even, on occasion, having orgasms! Lots of orgasms.

It's no accident that, when women discovered there was something in sex for them besides babies, horse racing dropped to second place and lovemaking leaped out in front to become the nation's number one sport. For good lovemaking enriches you emotionally and spiritually, relaxes muscles, makes you forget your worries for a while, aids in attaining restful sleep and is one of the few really beautiful and satisfying experiences in this world that isn't taxed.

The best benefit of all in lovemaking is that you are not alone. You have a companion who, if you chose well, admires you, enjoys you, knows how to take and give completely and is the kind of man who helps you build a bridge of intimacy that reaches into the heart, mind and soul of each of you.

That's the way it's supposed to be. But is that what's happening to you? Probably not. However, if you're not working with every ounce of you to make things that way, then you are depriving yourself unnecessarily, because *you can change your negative sexual and concomitant emotional pattern. I did, and so did a number of my friends.*

There are some lucky girls who come into full sexuality seemingly without effort but, for most, becoming a complete woman is a long and often arduous process. Very few of us succeed. Today's females are still being cheated and we know it. What's even more frustrating is that we, the victims, are being blamed for our predicament! And it's not our fault. We're *not* stupid or uninterested or lazy. It's simply that no one has ever told us explicitly how to go about becoming truly sensuous inside and out.

Even our own sex won't level with us. The women who have achieved that rarefied state of full sensuality have been as close-mouthed about how they did it as Jack Benny is with the combination to his underground vault.

Of course I can understand their silence. The shortage of really great males forces even the most desirable women to keep on their toes. Men are fragile creatures. If they survive being born, it's almost a sure thing they'll do themselves in too early in wars, in cars, in overwork or, if all else fails, by shoveling snow.

With the competition at such a fierce level, only a fool would share her secrets of success with a potentially sexy woman like you, but here I am revealing all. Someone must be spiking my Diet Rite cola with truth serum.

The main sources of information to date on female sexuality have been novels, marriage manuals and magazine articles, and a great many of them were written by men. The most important work on sex, *Human Sexual Response* by Masters and Johnson, tells how our

16

bodies behave in the act of love when we are responding correctly, but not how to achieve that correct response if we never have done so or if we have a very low response pattern.

For years my response pattern was so low you couldn't have picked it up on the most sensitive seismograph. Where were those strings of climaxes, seething passions and ecstatic moments I kept hearing so much about? Something seemed to be wrong with me. But what? Two psychologists told me I didn't have any mental blocks (about *sex,* that is). My gynecologist assured me my body was normal. If neither my mind nor body was at fault, then there had to be another key to sensuality for me.

My instinct kept telling me I *could* be a Sensuous Woman; there really *was* a torrent of passion pent up inside me waiting to be freed. Somehow or other, even without the experts, I was going to release that passion.

I wish I could say that my revelation of how to become a Sensuous Woman came to me while I was admiring Rodin's "Hand of God" at the Metropolitan Museum of Art, marveling at the Grand Canyon or walking through a redwood forest, but actually I was fighting a woman for a pair of blue silk sale shoes in Gim-

17

bel's basement when inspiration came. (I am one of the world's best department-store-sale in-fighters.) The shoes were a great bargain ($6.99 from $29.95 and in perfect condition) and, even though they give me blisters, I cherish them as a memento of that moment when I figured out the formula to awaken my body sexually.

Within six months of starting my sensuality program after the Gimbel's insight, I was satisfactorily sexually responsive and by the time the year was out I was reaching some real peaks of ecstasy. And were men courting me? You bet they were. It was heavenly. I had finally become a Sensuous Woman and it was just as fabulous as I thought it would be.

Now in case you think my sexual breakthrough was a fluke and won't work for anyone else, let me tell you about a few of my friends, starting with Carolyn (not her real name, of course), who happened to confess to me one afternoon over three Scotches and no lunch that it was her birthday, she was thirty-six years old, had been married twice, currently had a lover and *still* hadn't had one single, tiny orgasm in her whole life.

"It's not that my men haven't been good in bed," Carolyn moaned, "because they have

18

been. And my present lover is great. The hang-up is with me. But why? I feel affectionate, I enjoy sex, but no matter how hard I try, or don't try, I never catch on fire. I think I would sell my soul for one fantastic orgasm. I would give anything to know what it's all about."

Carolyn thought I was crazy when I told her about my secret sex program but, since she had nothing to lose, she decided to give it a try. Five weeks later she had her first orgasm and within several months she was able to come to climax with her lover most of the time.

One of the side benefits of Carolyn's breakthrough was that she felt so much more secure as a woman she stopped her nervous habit of biting her fingernails. Now she has hands pretty enough to appear in a hand lotion commercial (not for product X, mind you, but the *good* lotion).

"Hmm," I thought. "My program worked for me and was successful for Carolyn. Why wouldn't it help most women?" I began a few discreet test cases, like my former college roommate. Janet didn't have any trouble having an orgasm—one orgasm. But that was it. She found that my sensuality program enabled her to have two or three during a single love-

19

making session. Is she greedy? No, just happy. She enjoys the whole sex act more now, and her husband is unbelievably proud of himself because he can excite Janet so much. Uhmmhmmm. She lets him take all the credit. It makes him more eager to play.

Of course there is a lot more to sensuality than just orgasms, as my friend Grace discovered.

Grace is beautiful. In fact, there are some days it's just too depressing to be in the same room with her. She has long blonde hair; perfect features; big, green eyes; gorgeous skin; a thin, svelte body. She could be the girl in the Estée Lauder cosmetic ads. You wouldn't think anyone who looked like Grace could have man troubles, but she did. Her husband Bill had been spending more and more evenings at the office—you know, working late cleaning up all that paperwork. Grace knew the paperwork was another woman, but she didn't know what to do about it. When Grace learned how to satisfy Bill's craving for adventure (Chapter Thirteen), he took the early train home every night.

A couple more case histories of women I know well and then I'm going to help you learn for yourself.

Nothing much happened to my neighbor Kathy in bed because she didn't have time to get excited. Her husband was a five-minute man and, if that wasn't bad enough, he had the imagination of a gnat when it came to sexual variety. When Kathy began to experiment with the ecstasy-prolonging techniques I have detailed for you in Chapter Eleven, Harold started to last longer in bed and soon he was becoming downright adventurous in what he was doing to Kathy. She got Harold up to half an hour last month and is aiming for a full hour. Now that Kathy's so sensuous I wouldn't be surprised if she eventually lures Harold into a few two-hour lovemaking sessions.

My last example will be considered by many quite immoral, but you will have to admit Sue's immorality brought only happiness.

Sue is not particularly pretty. She is big-boned and chunky (even starvation diets leave her hefty), she's five feet ten in her stocking feet, nearly blind without her glasses and has, to put it delicately, a big nose. (I'm not being catty. That's Sue's own description of herself.) The only dates Sue could get were impossibles. I think she holds the Ohio record for sitting home alone on Saturday nights.

When Sue was twenty-five she took the three

thousand dollars she had saved from her job as a crackerjack secretary with an electronics firm and spent the summer in Italy. Where the American boys had thought Sue wasn't worth their time, the Italian men, who are notoriously enchanted with American women, thought Sue, if not exactly great, was at least worth their attention.

Sue had her first sexual experience in Palermo—and loved it. The next morning she deserted her travel group and started on a very special tour of her own. Instead of concentrating on Italy's museums and scenic wonders, Sue spent her summer in Italy's beds, learning everything she could about the art of pleasing a man sexually. She was an excellent student.

The Sue who reluctantly went home to Ohio that fall was a different girl. She looked about the same, but now there was a sensual aura about her that made two men decide they would like to take her out. Sue's talents in the bedroom drove both men nearly wild (yes, she was sleeping with two men concurrently). Did she marry either of them? No. And nothing bad happened to her in the way of punishment for her supposed wickedness. On the contrary, those two gentlemen fluttering around Sue served as an attention-getter that brought Jack into her web.

Jack ordinarily would never have looked twice at Sue, but he got so curious about what two first-rate men could see in such a homely girl that one night, when he had nothing better to do, he asked Sue to go to dinner with him. On their very first date, because he was really focusing on Sue, Jack realized that she was intelligent, nice and exceptionally good company. She found that, when she looked beyond his handsome exterior, Jack was a stimulating and bright man with a great sense of humor. They both found they shared such interests as Nero Wolfe mysteries, Renaissance art, ice skating, Jerry Lewis movies and (hmm) Italian food.

He asked her out again—and again.

When Sue finally allowed Jack to make love to her (she was in no hurry), it was like shooting a sitting duck. One evening of her artistry and he was hooked. They were married that spring. Now they have three children and a truly happy marriage.

Sensuality helped Sue get her dream man and it helps her hold on to him. If she hadn't had the courage to step outside the moral teachings of her family, Sue would never have gotten a chance at Jack because he wasn't initially smart enough to see for himself that she was very special. He had to have two other men point it out to him.

Now I didn't teach Sue anything. Just the reverse. She was kind enough to pass on to me a few of her sensational man-holding techniques (you'll find them in Chapters Eight, Eleven and Thirteen). I tried them and so should you. Your man will be back for more.

Viva Italy!

Has anyone tried my sensuality program and failed? Yes, one. Who was it? Never mind. I promised you no more case histories in this chapter and I'm sticking to that promise! Besides, I don't believe she *really* concentrated and did everything exactly the way I told her to!

Now I would like your full attention for a moment. I know much that you will read in this book will seem, at best, a little kooky to you and, at the very least, exotic. If someone had handed me *The Sensuous Woman* a few years ago, I would have regarded it with caution.

But remember this. *The Sensuous Woman* worked for me, a number of my friends and some of *their* friends. I think it will work for you too, and I hope you will give it a good try.

When you have completed that long trip from lousy sex to great sex, you will find it was worth the work.

For have you forgotten that all-important benefit I mentioned in paragraph nine? Men. Interesting men, sexy men. Because men with something on the ball can't resist the challenge and the tantalizing possibilities of the Sensuous Woman.

Your sex life and your love life can be everything you want them to be. No matter how hopeless you feel now, as you try the program in this book, you will be surprised at how your life picks up.

You want to be a full woman, don't you? Then down to business.

2

Sex—It's All in Your Head: You Can Learn to Be Sensuous

Everything you have done in this life you have *learned* to do. That pretty head of yours has been the control tower that directed you to weed out, through reasoning, the wrong ways to accomplish a goal. It has led you on to walk successfully for the first time—to talk, read, write, sing, swim, balance your checkbook, play bridge, master the intricacies of grocery shopping on a budget. It has even helped you

26

acquire the art of putting on false eyelashes.

Your control tower is also going to teach you to be a Sensuous Woman. All you have to do is relax, clear your head of those preconceived notions that have been stumbling blocks to sensuality and open yourself up to new signals.

I don't care if you are built like a truck driver or Twiggy or look like Bette Davis in *Whatever Happened to Baby Jane?* No excuses. You *can* attract a man worth your attention, drive him wild with pleasure and keep him coming back eagerly for more.

How exactly (yes, I did promise to be explicit) are you going to work this miracle? Forget all that nonsense you've read about a fancy new make-up job, or a wondrous girdle that makes you look slim and taut and zingy (you have to take it off to make love, remember) or a hypnotic perfume that draws him irresistibly to you.

You're not going to become a Sensuous Woman by painting and prodding your exterior, but by digging up and honing a lot of qualities that have been lying fallow deep within you.

There are four keys to sensuality:

27

1. Heightened sensitivity.
2. Appetite.
3. The desire to give.
4. Sexual skill.

In this and the next chapter we will concentrate on the first key—heightened sensitivity.

In lovemaking your body is your instrument. You shouldn't settle for less than the best. An Artur Rubinstein or Van Cliburn is not going to select a clunky, unresponsive, out-of-tune piano on which to perform his artistry.

I assume you want a first-rate lover. Then realize that no man is going to play the game of love with you very long unless you can make him feel like he is a Rubinstein on a good day.

So we're going to turn you into a concert grand. You may feel like a stiff, squeaky spinet at the moment, but be patient. The exercises in this chapter and the next will start you on your way toward becoming a sexy new Steinway.

I might as well warn you right now before you read any further that I'm deadly serious about these exercises. They may seem silly to you at first, but that's only because you've never seen anything like them. After a while you're not going to look or feel any more ridiculous doing them than when you massage your tired and aching feet after standing on them all day or are caught doing your derrière-firm-ing exercises or catch sight of yourself in the mirror with your face slathered in cold cream and your hair caught in clusters of rollers.

Sensuality Exercise Number One

This first exercise is to make you more aware of your tactile sense. Gather together a number of household items with different textures, like a leather glove, powder puff, cracker, bar of soap, rolling pin, fur hat, dish of tepid water, terry cloth towel, your wig, silk scarf, slice of bread, velveteen pin cushion, piece of lace, feathers, pearl necklace, leaf of a plant and whatever else you fancy, and place them on a table. Dim the lights. Sit down in a comfort-able chair, blindfold yourself and then *slowly and gently* run your hands over the items for approximately ten minutes. Let each one's spe-cial texture imprint itself on your fingertips.

Now lean back in the chair and re-create in your mind the feel of each item so that your fingers actually memorize the cool firmness of the pearls, the rough intricacy of the lace, the bumpiness of the cracker, the airiness of the powder puff, the unexpected firmness of the velveteen. You'll be surprised at your tactile memory.

Touch everything one more time and then rest.

Sensuality Exercise Number Two

Remove the clothes on the upper part of your body. Sit down at the table again and, with your eyes closed, take items like the fur and the feather and the towel and one by one softly caress your body in this order: Take the item in your right hand, start with the tips of the fingers on the left hand and draw the fur, the feather, the towel or whatever v-e-r-y slowly up the palm, the wrist, the inside of the arm to the neck, the left cheek, the forehead, across the eyelids, the nose, right cheek, mouth, neck, down to the shoulders, across the chest, over and under the breasts and back to the table. Sit back a moment, still with your eyes closed, and memorize the sensations you just stimulated on your body.

With the next item, reverse the hand that holds and strokes. You will know you are doing this exercise properly when your skin begins to tingle and feel the imaginary imprint of the item.

30

Sensuality Exercise Number Three

This one is most effective just before retiring for the night.

Put fresh sheets on the bed, spray them lightly with your favorite perfume or cologne, turn off the electric lights and light a candle and put your favorite romantic music on the record player or find a station on your radio that plays soothing music.

Now take a long, hot bath, letting yourself relax physically and unwind mentally. Dry yourself off with the towel as if you were blotting a six-hundred-year-old Ming Dynasty vase and stretch out naked on the newly made bed.

Let the flickering of the light, the softness of the music, the femininity of the scent, the bare freedom of your body ooze into you.

Roll over—
Stretch out—
Curl up—
Arch your back—
Wiggle your toes.

Then, take your favorite hand or body lotion, pour a tiny, icy pool of it between your breasts and over your abdomen. Close your eyes and, with delicate firmness, massage the liquid into your warm and thirsty skin. Take your time. Luxuriate in the sensation of your hands lovingly tending to all the curves and mounds of your body.

Does this sound like I'm trying to turn you into a narcissist? To a certain extent, yes. Until you can really rejoice in the uniqueness of your own body, you won't be able to give yourself fully in a lovemaking situation. Just because you aren't built like Raquel Welch doesn't mean that you aren't very special indeed. Your newly perceptive way of touching should help you discover and take pride in your own quite remarkable construction.

Finished rubbing in the lotion? All right. Blot any excess off with a towel, blow out that candle, turn over and go to sleep. If you have done this exercise properly, you should fall asleep more easily and wake up with silkier skin.

Sensuality Exercise Number Four

One of the most important parts of the body in lovemaking is the tongue. If you're much of a talker at all, this organ is already quite flexible, but you will be amazed at how the following exercises will increase that flexibility and also strengthen the tongue.

1. Stick your tongue straight out as far as you can. Then slide it back into your mouth as far as it will go. Do this exercise five times.
2. Try to touch your nose with your tongue— five times.
3. Try to touch your chin with your tongue— five times.
4. Encircle your lips in a clockwise motion with your tongue five times and then reverse the motion to counter-clockwise five times.

Try to work up to a count of twenty-five times with each exercise over a period of a month.

Sensuality Exercise Number Five

For this one you will need a truly delicious prop—a double dip ice cream cone. Remember that erotic eating scene in the movie *Tom Jones?* Well, you can do a great deal with your tongue on that cone in the way of sensuous action. Make circle and swirling patterns with your tongue on the ice cream, lap at it delicately like a kitten with milk, put all of your mouth over the ball of ice cream, sliding down until your lips touch the cone and then s-l-o-w-l-y withdraw it. When the ice cream starts to melt in rivulets down the side of the cone, catch the drops on the tip of your tongue. Linger over each morsel of ice cream, letting your taste buds fully savor the flavor, texture and cold.

Sensuality Exercise Number Six

The tongue again, and this is the wildest one yet. Close your eyes, lean back, relax. Now run your tongue over the tips of your fingers, down around the palm, circling the hollow of the palm; move down to your wrist and up your arm to the elbow. Feel those crazy sensations? If not, you haven't done your work properly on Exercises 1 and 2. Go back to the beginning and concentrate! (A word of caution here. I *do not* recommend doing Exercise Number 6 immediately after Exercise Number 3.)

Sensuality Exercise Number Seven

Exercise Number 7 is a reading and working assignment. Rather than try to describe to you those all-important sexercises to condition your lovemaking muscles, such as the gluteals, abdominals and levator, I strongly advise you

34

to read and *do* the exercises recommended by Bonnie Prudden, America's foremost physical fitness expert, in her book *How to Keep Slender and Fit after Thirty*. Although you can benefit from the whole book, the sexercises are contained in Miss Prudden's remarkable seventh chapter. I think you'll find her healthy, no-nonsense attitude toward sex refreshing and the exercises fantastic. Don't procrastinate on that exercise program. You're really going to need those toned-up muscles when you get to Chapter Eleven where I describe how to do delicious things to the man you love.

Sensuality Exercise Number Eight

Dance. The old-fashioned way where he holds you in his arms. Let your body melt into his and let him lead completely as you concentrate on the feel of his body next to yours, the coordination of his muscles as he moves you around the floor. If you close your eyes it will help you tune out visual distractions and allow you to be aware only of him and the music.

This kind of dancing is good preparation for later. In lovemaking, the woman must be able to follow the man's lead and tune into his body rhythms and style. While occasionally nothing will delight him more than your taking the initiative, breaking rhythm and turning him into the follower, in the main he will not be happy unless he is controlling the lovemaking. He wants you to do everything imaginable to him, but he also wants to tell you when. Because we women know so much more about sex nowadays and are openly revealing our hungers and our knowledge, men are being put to a much tougher test, performancewise. Now, as never before, even the most fantastic lover needs to know that he is in full command of the scene sexually. If you learn to follow expertly, he will feel your appreciative response to his performance and outdo himself. So you see, by your letting him be a happier lover, he will be a better lover and you both will benefit.

So dance. It's such a romantic way to improve sexual technique—and the exercise is good for you.

Sensuality Exercise Number Nine

Go out and splurge on some absolutely scrumptious underthings—lacy, silky, meltingly feminine. Avoid that $2.99 table like the plague and indulge yourself in real quality and beauty. You and your body deserve it and oh,

what it does for you as a woman psychologi-
cally to know that hidden under your dress are
a petticoat so delicate and luxurious that Audrey Hepburn would crave it, an absolutely
weightless bra that contours your breasts to
their seductive best and elegantly wicked panties that make you feel like Elizabeth Taylor on
her way to meet Richard Burton.

I think you get the idea.

Sensuality Exercise Number Ten

This exercise is so important that I felt I had
better devote a whole chapter to it. So turn
the page to find out about the importance
of——

3

Masturbation

Making love is a physical endeavor and as such has much in common with football, baseball, swimming, golf and other sports. You may have a natural aptitude for swimming, say, but that aptitude will only start you on your way. To learn to swim well and for long periods of time you must train your body to endure and thrive with a regular regimen of exercises tailored to improving lung power, muscle tone and technique.

If you visited a football or baseball training camp you would be dumbfounded at all the calisthenics and bone-crushing exercises the men must do daily before they are even allowed to get *near* the playing field. Until their bodies are strong and responsive, their reflexes as highly charged as Elvis Presley's when he is singing "Hound Dog," they aren't allowed to get into a practice game, much less the real thing.

So must it be with you.

To awaken your body and make it perform well *you must train like an athlete for the act of love.*

Your training camp is the privacy of your bedroom. Your exercises are the nine in the previous chapter and the crucial tenth exercise (with its many variations) outlined in this chapter.

Sensuality Exercise Number Ten is masturbation.

I know. It's supposed to be very wicked. But it isn't a bit evil, and don't you let anyone tell you it is.

Masturbation is an awkward, ugly, socially unutterable word for one of the most gratifying human experiences. It is wholesome, normal and sound, yet the word itself has an unwholesome, abnormal and embarrassing taint to it. Women who will admit to an affair, with only a twinge of self-consciousness, will huffily deny any personal knowledge of this most common sexual act and imply that only a few unfortunate and sexually aberrated women are driven to the extremes of masturbation.

Yet nearly every woman masturbates at some time in her life.

Smart women masturbate quite a lot, because they have discovered that it opens the doors of sensuality to them, for it strengthens and increases the flexibility of the love muscles, helps the body to coordinate fully at demand and teaches women to have orgasms—many orgasms—easily.

When you think of all it can do for you, isn't it worth overcoming your revulsion toward the word—and the act?

Masturbation workouts will teach you which places of your body arouse the most pleasure in you when caressed, what kind of manipulation in the clitoral area gives you the quickest response and/or the most exquisite one, what your multiple-orgasm pattern is (must you stop for a minute before going on or are you able to continue manipulation and go immediately to the next orgasm?). You will learn how many orgasms you can have in a single session before tiring. Some women are satisfied with three or four; a few have gone as high as a hundred before wearing out!

Now if you are groaning that I'm taking all the romance out of sex and turning it into something mechanical and inhuman, you couldn't be more wrong. If you can teach your body to reach orgasm in three minutes, say, just think what that responsive body of yours is going to do and feel when *he* is caressing it! How much more delicious to become fully erotic immediately than wasting that precious lovemaking time with him *trying* to come alive. In a few months of work you should be able to have several orgasms with him in the time it takes you now to feel the first real glow of arousal.

The reason *you* have to teach yourself to come alive is that men don't have the patience to explore your body thoroughly while they are sexually excited themselves. They want to get on with the action, not play laboratory.

You, because you have an investment in discovering how to turn yourself on, will spend the necessary hours, days and weeks and, because he isn't around observing you, you won't feel self-conscious or pressured.

Are you ready?

Pick a time of day or evening when you are assured of lengthy privacy. Remove all your clothes, turn the bell off on your telephone, turn down the lights (or turn them off completely if it makes you feel more comfortable) and stretch out on the bed.

Close your eyes and mentally and then physically run your hands *slowly* over your body.

Now gently lubricate your clitoral and vaginal areas with vaseline, KY jelly, Nivea or any other convenient face and hand cream (although I would stay away from products containing hormones or other unusual additives). Take your time in applying the lubricant. Let your fingers explore the area. Is the head of the clitoris ultrasensitive to the touch? Do you get a warm, prickly sensation when you rub the shaft? Does it feel better on the right side? The left? Is the whole mons area beginning to feel tingly? As you massage the lubricant into the vaginal lips, do they seem to expand slightly?

No two women masturbate exactly alike. In the next sections I will describe some of the basic ways to masturbate. Try each of them several times, then pick the ones you like best and go on to develop variations of your own that are particularly pleasing to you.

Mechanical Manipulation

If you have never had an orgasm or if you have great difficulty in achieving orgasm, the vibrator will probably work wonders for you. There are many different kinds of vibrators on the market. In checking with a number of women, I found that the most popular style for masturbatory activity was a battery-operated (no worrying about becoming entangled in electric cords) vibrator, shaped rather like a penis. It is inexpensive and on display in most drug stores. It is an effective clitoral stimulator and can also be inserted into the vagina. Since the machine is advertised as a facial massager, you can purchase it without embarrassment. The sales clerk isn't going to know what *you* intend to use it for.

Another popular vibrator is a Scandinavian model that fits over the top of the hand, allowing the throbbing sensations to be transmitted to your body through your fingers instead of a rubber tip. This model is fairly expensive, but it is well constructed and effective.

There are a number of vibrators that come with three or four attachments, each giving a different set of sensations. If you shop around a little, you will find a vibrator that meets your needs and pocketbook.

Now to get down to the use of the vibrator. Remember, you are lying there quietly, eyes closed, tuning into the feel of your body.

Let your mind float to someone that excites you sexually. It could be anybody. A movie star, that handsome man ahead of you in line at the bank yesterday, the new executive in Personnel at the office, your boy friend, your neighbor down the street.

Imagine him looking at you stretched out naked on the bed, your body open and hungry for him. Feel him caressing your breasts, running his hands down and over your abdomen, stroking the inside of your thighs, reaching higher now and gently massaging your clitoris. Let the vibrator be his hands and penis. Take your time. You have all night to savor these sensations. Let yourself go. Be swallowed up in the continuous, rhythmic stimulation of the vibrator as it moves up and down and around your clitoris and vagina. Let your fantasy man rule your mind and body. Is he thrusting deep into you while your pelvis is arching up to him, aching for him, eager to explode in the commanding ecstasy of orgasm? Is he teasing you, making you reach out for the next tantalizing sensation? If one fantasy doesn't work for you, wander lazily on to another. You have hours of sensuality to relish.

If you have trouble conjuring up a fantasy, pick a sexy section from a book and re-read it while using the vibrator. Some of the literature that has turned on women I know are the lovemaking scenes in *Lady Chatterley's Lover*, sections of *The Story of O*, that scene in *Gone With the Wind* where Rhett Butler carried Scarlett up the stairs, parts of *The Love Pagoda*, *The Sheik*, *Fanny Hill* and *The Carpetbaggers*. You probably have others that are your special favorites.

Allow your fantasies to excite you. Some women have fantasies of being kidnapped and raped, being ravished by a tiger, being made love to by several men at once, having sex with a woman, etc. Be as outrageous in your fantasy selection as you like. After all, no one is ever going to know unless *you* tell.

A number of women don't begin to experiment with masturbation until they are in their twenties or even thirties. If you are a beginner at masturbation and orgasms, you may not strike it rich the first time out. It could take a few weeks of practice to get your body to respond freely. Also, those unused muscles are going to be creaky and sore in the beginning. You will have to build up their strength by repetition. Remember how it felt when you rode a bicycle again after not using those muscles since you were a child? Ouch.

The main thing the beginner must have is patience, for you will succeed. Sexual research has shown that ninety-five percent of women who use self-stimulation become orgasmic. With the use of the vibrator you will probably in a few weeks' time be able to have an orgasm within one minute of contact and go right on to several more.

Hand Manipulation

Once you have mastered the vibrator, you should move on to the use of your hands. Now that you know what an orgasm feels like, it is time to expand your ability to achieve full arousal and orgasm with a less probing touch. The vibrator will have spoiled you, and it will be harder to transfer your response pattern to the less stimulating manipulation of your fingers, but persevere, because you are teaching yourself to reach a higher plateau of sensitivity. With your hands you will discover shadings of sensation you would never know existed with the vibrator.

Every woman develops her own individual masturbation style, according to Dr. William Masters and Mrs. Virginia Johnson (*Human Sexual Response*), but there are some practices common to most females. Women rarely directly manipulate the head of the clitoris, as the sensation there can be too intense, causing the clitoris to become painful or irritated. Instead, women usually concentrate on the right side of the clitoral shaft, if they are right-handed, or the left if they are left-handed, or they stimulate the entire mons area with circular, press and release, up and down, fast or slow movements or whatever is most pleasing. It takes longer to come to orgasm with mons manipulation, but it is just as satiating an experience as direct clitoral shaft massage. It's all a matter of personal preference and only you, through experimentation, will be able to find what you like best.

As you continue to practice hand manipulation, you will find that you are cutting down the time it takes you to get to orgasm and you will have discovered how to keep manipulating yourself to achieve those multiple orgasms. *Set aside several hours a week for masturbation so your new response pattern will become a stable one.* Remember, you are training your body to become a superb instrument of love. You'll never accomplish that with sporadic lessons. You can't learn to play the piano if you only go near it a few times a year. If you masturbate only once or twice a month you can't possibly expect your body to learn and retain much.

Masturbate to your heart's content. After you have become accustomed to it, keep adding to the number of orgasms you achieve in each session. The minimum you should settle for is three or four and you should try for ten to twenty-five. You can't hurt yourself. When your body has had enough, it will cry "exhaustion!" and you will know to stop.

When you have educated your body to the point where it can reel off several orgasms at your command, you will be able to guide him when you are making love to positions that give you the maximum sensation. After all, if *you* don't know what sets your body off sensually, how can you expect *him* to know? Every woman is different, and he's not clairvoyant.

There are an almost unending number of ways to masturbate. You are limited only by your imagination and inclination. Here are some I have heard about. Some I have tried, some I haven't.

Water Manipulation

The Jacuzzi whirlpool bath is heavenly. Just lie back in a bubble bath, direct the stream of water from the machine at your clitoris and enjoy, enjoy.

I'm told you can get a similar effect from the new bidets. Place yourself backward on the toilet seat and adjust the spray so that it hits the spot that excites you the most.

Ready for another? Remove the head from the shower, turn on the water and adjust the pressure and temperature so that it will be comfortable on your genitals, lie down in the tub on your back and angle your clitoral area into position to receive the weight and sensation of the stream of water.

You can also get some interesting sensations from hand showers and the spray from garden hoses, I'm told.

Variant Manipulation

Many girls insert objects into their vaginas to simulate the feel and movement of the penis. Some of the more popular objects are candles, hot dogs, bananas, sausages and, of course, those big rubber penises that are offered for sale by a number of mail order houses. For heaven's sake, though, do be bright about it. *Don't* use coke bottles, test tubes or splintery wooden things. You won't enjoy it when the doctor has to pick out all those broken pieces.

I've heard, but haven't had it authenticated, that you can get an orgasm horseback riding.

Then there's the Chinese Tickle. You take three silver balls, insert them in your vagina and then use a vibrator on the outside of the vagina. Apparently the vibrator makes the balls jump around like mad and it's supposed to be a very exciting sensation.

The most unusual way of masturbation that I've heard of to date is to pop your clothes into the automatic washer, turn it on and then plaster your pelvis to the machine so that the pulsations from the machine's cycles give you a few tremors of your own.

Next someone will figure out how to get orgasms from computers.

There are many, many ways to masturbate. Before long you'll probably be writing me telling *me* how.

I am completely sold on the value of masturbation to teach your body to be sexually responsive. It worked for me and for many other women. If you will really concentrate and devote enough time to it, I feel sure it will open the doors of sexuality for you too.

Come on now and try it. It won't take you long to realize that masturbation is a happy, healthy, normal act that can contribute to your well being and sensuality enormously.

By the way, masturbation can also be an effective control. If you are sexually uptight and you find the selection of sexual partners available to you distinctly unappetizing, you can avoid an experience you will later regret by getting your release without complication.

Masturbation also has another benefit that surprised me enormously. Masters and Johnson discovered in their research with forty-three women using automanipulative techniques that strong orgasmic experience shortly after the beginning of menstruation "increased the rate of flow, reduced pelvic cramping when present and frequently relieved their menstrually associated backaches."

Now will you believe me when I say masturbation is good for you?

4.

The *Single* Woman:
Does She or Doesn't She?

Is it the end of the world if just about every-body suspects you have a sex life?

No. Not if you are an adult.

When you grew up you put the things of childhood away. One of those was virginity.

Was there anything wrong with people be-ing aware as you came into womanhood that you developed breasts, rounded hips, pubic hair and a thoroughly female body? Of course not. Then what is wrong in people assuming you would use your matured female equipment as it was designed to be used—for lovemaking and childbearing? Be proud that you function as a woman and don't let the fear of negative public opinion deter you from becoming a full woman.

Now I know a few people are going to try to beat you down and force you into a corner marked "shame," if you don't play the virgin role. But you don't have to abide by their rules. Every woman has an inner voice that will tell her honestly what is right or wrong for her. If you tune into that voice and follow it, you will handle your sex life well.

Our world has changed. It's no longer a question of "Does she or doesn't she?" We all know she wants to, is about to or does. Now it's only a question of how tastefully she goes about it.

5.

Maintenance, Reclamation and Salvage

We both know that when you're marketing a product (you), packaging is important. Unless you catch the buyer's eye, you'll never be taken off the shelf. That doesn't mean you have to be beautiful, but you had better be attractive and have individuality. You'll never get into the shopping cart, much less his home, unless you appear interesting.

Most of the pointers listed below, you already know about, so I have not gone into detail. If you are slipping in any of these areas, regard my comments as signposts of danger and start *today* to correct your carelessness.

Let's Start with Your Appearance

You must devote a great deal of your time to finding the clothes that flatter you. Pore over the fashion magazines, study women whose taste you admire, try on many different styles in the department stores. If you've always wondered what you would look like in a black velvet jump suit or a slinky cashmere dress, don't wonder. Try them on and see for yourself.

Learn your figure faults and then try to steer the eye away from them. I have a small waist and wide hips, for instance, which means you'll never catch me in a straight or pleated skirt. Instead I look for dresses with a soft flare or an A line and shift my area of accent to the neck with a flattering collar or beautiful scarf. If you have a great bustline but fat legs, burn your textured stockings and go for dresses, sweaters and blouses in clinging fabrics and provocative styles that set off the wonders of your cleavage. If you're flat-chested but have divine legs, stay away from low necklines and wear the shortest skirts you can get away with and the sheerest or wildest hose and very feminine shoes.

Learn to follow fashion but don't let it enslave you. If this is the year that everyone is wearing sexy little black dresses, you wear sun gold. Just think how much more easily he'll be able to find you at that crowded cocktail party.

If this year's colors are sea green and pumpkin but he likes blue (and it happens to be most men's favorite color), wear plenty of blue.

Never buy a dress just because it is practical. Unless it makes you feel happy and very special, put it back on the rack.

Before you let them wrap up that yummy creation that's going to cost a week's salary or keep your family on casseroles for a month, be sure to sit down in it and study your reflection in the mirror. Does it pull, pucker, hike up? Walk around. Does the skirt keep you from moving gracefully? Raise your arms toward the ceiling. Is a sudden impetuous desire to wrap yourself around his neck going to cause an embarrassing rip? Bend over. Do the seams around your derrière look like they're trying to hold back the Johnstown flood?

Clothes that don't fit properly are not sexy.

Find out what colors are flattering to you and then *wear them*. Give that sensible mud brown dress that makes your complexion look like death to the Salvation Army and buy that blush pink gown that makes your skin glow.

Work like the devil to accent your good features and hide the bad. Now don't tell me you don't have any good features because I don't believe you. Look again. How about your eyes, your teeth, your feet, your hair? Do you have a beautiful back, a provocative behind?

If you are guilty of this one, shame and double shame: *Don't ever let a man catch you in underthings held together by safety pins.*

Make-up can be a woman's ally or enemy, depending on the skill and taste of the applier. Properly used, make-up will enhance your looks. Applied improperly it can make you look like an escapee from a side show. If you're not sure that what you are doing is right for you, there are several places to get help. Many of the ultra-chic beauty salons have a resident expert. Most department stores invite make-up experts to visit their stores and advise you how to apply make-up, what foundation is right for your skin tone, how to play up your beautiful features and play down the bad. There are also several magazines which have monthly articles on make-up, and there are a number of good books. My favorite is *Look Like a Star* by TV make-up expert Ray Voege, who's spent twenty years making a lot of famous people look glamorous in front of the camera. Mr. Voege also has a chapter on make-up problems and solutions unique to the black woman. Why is this book my favorite? Because it removes the mumbo-jumbo from the cosmetic field and doesn't try to convince you that you have to apply one hundred and sixty-two products to your weary face before you dare walk out on the street.

Canvass your town until you find a man who is an expert at haircutting and then gratefully pay any exorbitant sum he wishes to extract from you. The crucial factor in how your hair will look daily is not the woman who bows your head down with three dozen rollers and then bakes you under the dryer once a week, but that basic cut. If it isn't right, no set is going to hold its shape and continually flatter your face and look fresh and neat every day.

Unless your man is allergic to it, do wear perfume. Finding the right one will take some experimenting. You'll know you've hit it when several people tell you that you smell heavenly today and what's the name of your perfume, because they want to get some for their girl friends or their wives.

Be sure that your fingernails and toenails are always well manicured and that your polish isn't chipped. Men as a rule don't like those overly long Dragon Lady nails, so check out your man's taste before you go for that spiky look.

Even if your style is a tousled one, you must be neat in your appearance. No sagging slips or petticoats, runs in your hose, bedraggled gloves, scuffed shoes with run-down heels, blouse half hanging out, scruffy handbag, missing buttons on your coat, threads dangling from your hem, yesterday's make-up congealing on your face. If your blouse or dress has ineradicable stains on it or is faded, throw it away or wear it only when you're cleaning out the basement.

My last bit of advice on appearance is: Do try to wear shoes that don't hurt. It improves your disposition so.

Cleanliness

While many European men seem to be rather disinterested in cleanliness, American men favor women who take baths. If you're inclined to dip your body into the H_2O only when you reach an emergency condition, you're not going to be in demand for anything much besides cleaning out pigsties.

Bathe often. Use a deodorant. Remove excess hair from your armpits and lower legs. If you have a mustache, get electrolysis treatments. Keep your fingernails and toenails clean. Shampoo your hair until it squeaks.

During your periods be sure you change your sanitary napkins and tampons often enough so there is no chance of odor build-up. Ugh. Smelling in a love area is not sexy.

If you're troubled with vaginitis (all women are at one time or another) see your gynecologist.

The one area of the body that women forget to clean is the clitoris. Because of its design, little particles are easily trapped there and remain hidden from view. Pull back the skin and gently rinse out the exposed area daily.

Get a Water-Pik. You'll find your teeth will be cleaner than they ever have been in your life and your mouth fresher It's also great for your gums.

Your Figure

Take it off. If you're harboring a bunch of fat, it's going to keep you from getting as close as you want to the man in your life. If you're having trouble removing the excess weight yourself, go to an expert in obesity. He'll tailor a diet to your particular needs, and the fact that you have to report in to him every week acts as a spur to discipline. If there isn't a good doctor near you, try Weight Watchers. They have helped people melt off tons of fat.

While it's true he may love you with that extra fifteen pounds jiggling around on you, he'll love you more and be *prouder* of your appearance if you shed that blubber.

If you're not overweight but just flabby or poorly proportioned, then exercise. Yes, I know. I hate it, too. But it seems to be a fact of our underactive lives. Again, I recommend the Bonnie Prudden book *How to Keep Slender and Fit After Thirty* for women of all ages, and she has an almost painless exercise album out called "Keep Fit/Be Happy" (Warner Brothers). There are also exercise programs available at your local YWCA.

As grisly as exercise is, it will shape you up, help you shed that tired feeling and improve your posture.

Your Health

Be sure to go to your gynecologist twice a year and your regular doctor once a year for checkups. Unless you are healthy you aren't going to enjoy sex.

Your Voice

There is nothing more abrasive in a woman than an irritating voice. You can look like Gina Lollobrigida, but if you sound like a fingernail screeching across a blackboard when you open your mouth, he's going to want to spend as little time in your company as possible. Many women are blissfully unaware that they have ugly voices. Borrow a tape recorder or use an office dictaphone and *listen* to yourself. Is that voice you hear soft, feminine, musical? Or is it raspy, harsh, too loud? You can spend the whole afternoon at the beauty salon getting yourself gorgeous, but what have you gained if every time you whisper sweet nothings in his ear he flinches?

If you do have a voice that you feel can stand improvement (and who doesn't?), it's usually not difficult to dig up a competent speech therapist who will give you some exercises to smooth off your rough edges. Nearly all colleges and some high schools have speech therapists now, and usually your County Medical Association knows of someone in your area.

Is it worth all that work? Certainly. If, when you talk to him on the telephone your voice makes him want to come right over and caress you, you've achieved something really worthwhile, right?

Remember, all the sex goddesses of our times have had voices as interesting as their exteriors. Marilyn Monroe had a memorable breathy and vulnerable whisper. Sophia Loren's voice is tingly and velvety. Elizabeth Taylor's tiny voice exudes lustiness. Those women *learned* to sound like that. You, too, can have a distinctive and man-catching voice if you want one, and you should want one! Work at it.

The Hazards of Sex

There is no denying that there are risks involved in lovemaking.

Carelessness can cause an unwanted pregnancy.

Your husband or lover can give you a venereal disease. The very thought of syphilis or gonorrhea makes my stomach turn over and probably gives you the same reaction. It's a horrible infection to catch—but not the worst thing that could happen to you in this life. You're taking far greater risks smoking cigarettes than making love because you have the good luck to be having a sex life at a time when medical science is able to knock out that venereal disease in rapid order.

I would hardly call syphilis and gonorrhea status-symbol diseases, but a number of famous and highly respectable people have been stricken with them. Why, just the other day I was reading the biography of Jenny Churchill and much to my surprise it was mentioned that her husband, Lord Randolph (Winston's father), had had syphilis.

If you do get a sore or a discharge or the feeling that something is wrong in the genital area, don't sit around frozen in fear, run to your gynecologist and get fixed up. The longer you wait, the harder venereal diseases are to detect and cure.

Cry "help" to the doctor and "murder" to the man who gave it to you—but don't let those nosy neighbors hear you. The day hasn't quite arrived when venereal diseases are something to brag about.

Venereal disease is not the only disagreeable thing you can get from sexual intercourse. My best friend was having an affair with one of the most divine bachelors ever to grace the jet set (you'd know his name immediately) and in a romantic moment over strawberries and espresso at La Grenouille one spring evening he suggested they take a midnight flight to a charming villa he had at his disposal in the south of France. They went, the villa was indeed charming and the sixteenth-century beds the kind you sink into and never want to get out of—that is, until they realized that one of those beds had given them crabs (members of the lice family that attach themselves to the pubic hairs of the woman and all over the man). She was absolutely shattered when her eyes focused on the sight of the loathsome parasites biting into her and, although they both got immediate and thorough treatment, it was weeks before she got rid of that itchy, crawly feeling and felt really clean again. Now when she travels she's inclined to favor antiseptic Hilton hotels over romantic but potentially buggy villas.

As unpleasant as venereal disease, crabs and unwanted pregnancies can be, the risks aren't adequate reasons for you to deprive yourself of a wonderful sex life. The chances of any of these calamities descending upon you are slight, and all are correctable. You're in greater danger driving your car to the supermarket.

So relax and make love.

6.

Your Sexual Appetite

Certainly you have a sexual appetite. If you didn't, you wouldn't have gotten yourself involved in such a funny-looking activity. I'm sure that if creatures from Mars or Venus were peering at us during intercourse they would laugh at our antics. If they could feel what we feel, though, you can bet they'd leap from those flying saucers into the sack immediately.

Most of the time, if you are a full woman,

you are bursting with sexual appetite, especially if you've reached your mid- or late thirties. It is then that you come into your sexual prime and, unless you get some debilitating illness, that prime of yours will stay with you as long as you live. If you are loving sex at age forty, you are still going to love it at ages sixty and eighty. And you thought you were just going to crochet potholders and watch re-runs of "I Love Lucy" on TV when you got old! Hah.

Sexual appetite is crucial to good lovemaking for two reasons: (1) It gives you the impetus to explore your man's body with your own, thereby exciting him into being a better lover and (2) it's what sparks you into reaching out for the physical pleasure you are entitled to.

Value your sexual appetite highly and learn to understand its many moods. Are you dormant at the beginning of your period perhaps, or maybe at your peak when you are menstruating? Low in the morning and high at night? Are you fiery in the early afternoon, tepid just after dinner? Do you wake up in the middle of the night aching for him? Are you most passionate around the fourteenth or fifteenth day of the month? If fatigue makes you go cold sexually, do you make sure to get in a half hour nap on the days your man is likely to be in the mood for love? When you drink, have you learned to know when the liquor has ceased to be a stimulant and is about to turn you numb? Have you discovered what caresses unleash your sexual appetite and how to prolong or hurry sexual ecstasy?

As a woman, it is your responsibility to know fully the rhythms and whims of your body. If you've never paid attention, start today by keeping a little diary for the next three months. Note down the date and time of day when you become sexually excited and/or make love. After intercourse or masturbation, briefly rate your sexual response as superb, good, indifferent or lousy. You'll soon realize a great deal about yourself physically.

And then you will be able to appreciate and intelligently use your sexual appetite as it was intended to be used: as a crucial key of good lovemaking.

7.

Sexual Ethics

There is one bad feature to becoming a Sensuous Woman. You have to take the responsibility for your actions.

There will be times when you will be tempted to get involved with a man and be worried about whether he is right or wrong for you ethically.

I have developed my own set of ethics, which over the years have made a few "Should I or shouldn't I encourage him?" decisions easier to reach. I pass them on to you as food for thought.

1. I believe a woman must keep her hands off her sister's and best friend's men.
2. I believe it is immoral for a woman to let a man she doesn't like touch her—even if that man is her husband.
3. I believe it is immoral for a woman not to give herself completely to a man she loves (unless she has had the poor judgment to fall in love with a man who's bad for her—then she should run a mile from him).
4. I believe it is moral for a woman to give herself to a man she respects, likes and is sexually attracted to, as long as she doesn't betray a promise of fidelity she has made to another man.
5. I believe a woman has a moral obligation not to tease, lead on or in other ways emotionally and physically torture a man whose love and sexuality she cannot return.

Becoming a Sensuous Woman does not give you a license to do anything you please. Somewhere along the line you are going to have to arrive at a set of ethics that are workable. The earlier you become clear in your mind about what is right and wrong for you, the earlier you will save yourself a lot of nagging guilts and unpleasant situations.

8.

Sex—What to Wear

Now that we have rehearsed your body to the point where it knows all its lines and cues by heart, it's time to costume you and move you into the sexual arena.

Clothes

Men are unbelievably puzzling, stubborn, highly individual and at times really in horrible taste when it comes to how they want their ladies to look in bed. That stunning new peignoir that you bought because you thought it was seductive may, to him, just look "very nice," while the nothing little print sundress you got in Jamaica may transform him into a sex fiend. You're going to have to be a bit of a detective to discover just what boudoir attire excites each particular man and then adapt yourself to that style, for a man's idea of what is sexy can be enlarged upon but not often completely changed.

I think it must be obvious to you that if you are intending to have a frequent sex life you had better not slide between the sheets at night when *he's* around, covered with gooey creams, your hairdo protected by a beehive of toilet paper or bound up in curlers and your body draped in a baggy, faded old nightgown with a drooping hem and tattered trim. Only a gorilla, a sex fiend or a man deprived of sex for some time could get aroused in those circumstances.

On the other hand, going to bed wearing special night make-up and yards of provocative black lace is no guarantee of lovemaking either. If your man happens to go for the snow queen type, slinky black isn't going to turn him on.

There are two ways to discover how he envisions a sex goddess; one is to ask him directly and the other is to experiment with different looks. I favor a combination of both tactics, for obviously his description of what stimulates him visually is invaluable to you in winning and keeping him and, by experimenting with different looks from time to time, you will be effectively using a potent weapon—surprise. More on that later.

First, let's take a look at a few of the classic boudoir fashions.

An astonishing number of men find black garter belts, high heels and sheer black stockings highly erotic. I personally think they look garish, but, if the man I love wanted me to wear that get-up, I would from time to time and so should you. After all, no one else is going to see you and, if the picture of you prancing around like an escapee from a decadent French film makes him want to pull you into bed, it's pretty silly of you not to fan and benefit from his desire to sweep you away in a plethora of sensuality.

Many men are swayed by the snow queen

75

look—yards and yards of virginal white edged in lace or ruffles, with maybe a blue moiré sash, the setting a canopy or elegant Empire bed covered with embroidered sheets, white satin coverlets and piles of pale silk pillows. The challenge of arousing and conquering icy, feminine, perfect *you* can become a fever to this kind of man. He will usually be an exceptionally ardent lover and buy you expensive trinkets.

Great numbers of men still hanker for the traditional diaphanous black nightgowns. Almost invariably during the early years of marriage a wife will receive at least one seductive black nightie as a Christmas present from her husband. Don't say "Ugh! How revolting!" Be flattered that, instead of picturing you bent over the sink scrubbing last night's hash off the Revere Ware, he envisions you naked, except for an ounce or two of black nylon, curled up on the bed smoldering like Sophia Loren or Ava Gardner. Black nightgowns mean he's interested in sex and willing to spend some effort making it exciting.

If you are given completely wicked nightwear, blush if you must, but wear it with pride —and *often*. If he gives you a nightgown suitable for his great-grandmother, *then* you should start to worry, for you're in trouble as a woman.

Although those fluffy, short baby doll outfits are pretty much out of fashion at the moment, they do have their male fans, usually men that like to spoon-feed you caviar and ice cream, pet you and buy you huge, stuffed animals. If you crave feeling like a pampered child, try the baby doll look on him and see if he is your Sugar Daddy.

Another popular boudoir style is the well-scrubbed, just coming into young womanhood look. This is most effective if you have long, straight hair and wear simple, pristine but feminine nightgowns in pastels or tiny flower prints. Do keep an eye on the calendar though, and get the man you love hooked on another image of you as quickly as possible, because that young womanhood look is hell to pull off when you hit your thirties and forties. Let's not even *discuss* the fifties!

Of course one of the most sexually stimulating visions he can have when you re retiring for the night is you, popping into bed, perfumed, powdered and *naked*. If you have a good figure, the most attractive thing you can sleep in is your own skin.

Hair

Ever since women began bobbing their hair in the 1920's, men have been complaining. They are right. Long hair *is* sexy on the pillow, wonderful to run your hands through and great looking streaming down your back when you are nude. If your face and figure are enhanced by long hair *do* grow it, but if you look terrible in long tresses or just can't grow a healthy head of hair, don't feel depressed. Some of our greatest sex goddesses have had medium-length or even *short* hair—like Ava Gardner, Marilyn Monroe, Jane Russell, Simone Signoret and Jean Harlow.

Long hair, like perfect features, is desirable but not essential to attract a man.

You can, of course, resort to falls, hairpieces and wigs to please the hair-mad man. All that false hair can be marvelously sensual when he's admiring you from across the dinner table or devouring your profile in the flickering light of the movie house, but oh, the problems that can arise when he takes you and that hair to bed.

Wigs slip. The first time I tried to make love with a wig on, I spent most of my time clutching it frantically to keep it from turning completely around on my head. I have freed my hands for more interesting activities since that first horrible experience by firmly anchoring the wig to my scalp with a mountain of bobby pins, but I still regard lovemaking in a wig as something to be done on occasion—not regularly—because wigs get hot when you do and that expensive set melts. I'd rather mat my own hair. But a wig is fun every now and then, especially if it's a different color from your own hair, for it allows him to live out (with no threat to you) one of man's common fantasies —that he's making love to someone new and mysterious.

Falls and hairpieces have their built-in booby traps too. My friend Clare, who has a chestnut-brown fall that makes her look simply ravishing, had never let her new beau see her without it. He assumed all that hair was hers. The first time they made love, in an excess of passion he grabbed her by the hair to pull her down beside him and the hair came away in his hand. They both nearly fainted. He, because for one terrible moment he thought he had somehow inadvertently scalped her and she, because of embarrassment and because it hurt.

79

No matter if your hair is three inches or three feet long, men like to touch it and run their fingers through it. All men dislike oily hair and are vehement against excessive hair spray and hair styles so ornate that the man is afraid to touch the girl. So save those elaborate coiffures for the photographer, ladies' luncheons and charity benefits. They don't belong on a pillow. You, if you think about it, are the one to suffer the most from a fancy set, because if you are afraid of ruining it, you won't be able to relax and enjoy yourself in bed.

Women aren't the only vulnerable ones in the fake hair department. My friend Linda got her fingers stuck in the glue of her new boy friend's toupee (she hadn't realized he wore one). A touchy situation, you will admit. But while the sticky discovery did cool her ardor for the moment, she thought he looked just fine without his hair and made his secret work to her benefit. He was a well-known television announcer, and wherever they went in public they were plagued with well-wishers who just wanted to say "hello" but would then chatter on endlessly, shattering any mood and conversation she was enjoying with the announcer. Linda talked him into going out bareheaded (he really didn't look like the same man without the rug) and she had him all to herself in public and private.

He in turn was pleased and impressed over the fact that Linda was obviously dating the "real" him, not the celebrity on the television screen.

Bras

While we're dealing with fake coverings, we had better discuss the pros and cons of padded bras and falsies. I have a very definite opinion on this: Don't wear them to entice or seduce. When you take them off or out to make love, he'll see the real you and, if he's a breast man, he'll be disappointed. Wear your padded bras and falsies occasionally to enhance the lines of a specific dress or sweater and, if you are flat-chested, avoid men who are hooked on big breasts (they'll only give you an unnecessary inferiority complex) and find yourself a nice lover and/or husband who is crazy about your beautiful bottom, fantastic legs or whatever. After all, there is a big-breasted gal out there who's missing one or more of your good features and she needs the admiration of the big-breast fancier. You don't. For every man who loves big breasts there is another man who hates them (thank heavens!). Right?

Vision

Glasses are definitely out in bed, which until recently spoiled some of the pleasure for women who are nearly blind without their trusty spectacles. Being able to see your sexual partner, his facial expressions, how his body is reacting and those marvelous things he is doing to *you* are all part of the fun and stimulation of sex. If you've had the feeling lately you're making love to "The Shadow," get contact lenses. If you insert them properly before lovemaking, you'll see *everything* in exciting detail.

Make-up

I am of the school that believes you should scrub your face clean before you go to bed, yes, but leave on a trace of eyeliner and a touch of lipstick.

I look like a final-stage tuberculosis victim without a little color on my lips and, if my eyes aren't accented a trifle, they just completely disappear. A night of sleeping on my less-than-perfect face doesn't improve its appearance. *You* may wake up with shining eyes, a glowing skin and rosy cheeks. I wake up with circles under my eyes, pasty skin and a puffy face. Anything left over from the night before that will help disguise this I thankfully use. The only man who has ever seen my face completely bare is my doctor who, having picked a profession that brings people to him looking their worst, by now must be inured to gruesome sights.

Certainly we all know some women who look perfectly gorgeous without anything on their faces besides a dusting of powder, but even with plastic surgery I couldn't belong to that select group. So I color and highlight my face.

Many a woman is now putting *on* make-up before going to bed so that she not only looks her best while they're making love, but also will look good if he wakes up in the middle of the night and sees her sleeping away on the pillow next to him. Never thought of that horrible possibility, did you?

What do they wear? False eyelashes (no, I'm not kidding), eyeliner, an almost nonexistent foundation, a touch of rouge and lipstick. They'll spend half an hour putting on make-up designed to give the effect of no make-up at all.

Other women, who can't bring themselves to wear night make-up but still can't stand the idea of their men catching sight of them barefaced in the morning, always make sure to rise about fifteen minutes before their mates so that the circulation has a chance to begin to do its face-revitalizing work and they can peacefully and secretly apply that cheering bit of make-up.

Today there is only one situation a woman is forced to meet sans make-up—an operation —and several hospitals are beginning to relent a bit on their ridiculously rigid surgery rules. If ever there is a time when a woman needs her spirits lifted, it's when they're about to cut her open.

Do I ever completely remove all my make-up? Of course I do. Every day at least twice. But never when he's around. If he happened to come across me barefaced, I wouldn't have a nervous collapse, but I'm not looking for opportunities to display myself when I'm at my least attractive.

Pleasing the Polygamist

In a minute I'll get into the titillating possibilities of body paint and harem costumes, but first I think we ought to see why a woman should learn to be several different people for the man she loves.

Nearly all men are polygamous by nature. Yet they face the terrible frustration of living in a monogamous society. As much as I hate even to think about it, left to themselves most men would probably never marry. (To understand thoroughly this harsh fact, read Jim Moran's book *Why Men Shouldn't Marry*.) Therefore, it is natural for a man to have a wandering eye and a fertile sexual imagination. He's not betraying you when he looks longingly at that shapely blonde in the drugstore and dreams of devouring her. It's a natural instinct on his part and has nothing to do with the fact that he loves you very much. Married or not, men are going to continue looking, and a great number will sample women besides yourself. You may not like it, but you're going to have to live with it.

It's women who keep marriage alive and benefit most from it. So get this straight. *If she is going to keep her man monogamous, it's the woman's responsibility to give him the sexual variety and adventure at home that he could find easily on his own elsewhere.*

I know that's a tall order. You have to fight woman's most deadly sexual enemy—familiarity—for it breeds boredom in the male.

To keep him from wandering, your greatest allies are:

1. Imagination.
2. Sensitivity to his moods and desires.
3. The courage to experiment with new sexual techniques (Chapter Eleven), enticing situations and places.

Ready for examples? Ted and Marge have been married eight years. The first three, Ted was insane about Marge in bed, but during the fourth year Marge became aware that Ted didn't devote as much time to sex. Where they used to spend maybe an hour making love, they now had somehow slipped back to about half an hour. If that wasn't ominous enough, Marge began to realize that their lovemaking had a set pattern. She knew everything Ted was going to do before he did it and what her response would be. Instinctively Marge knew that Ted was ripe to fall into the bed of another woman because he needed the stimulation of a new experience. She determined that, to keep that other woman's hands off her Ted, she would rekindle his sex drive.

The next week Ted had to go to Pittsburgh on company business and, while he was away, Marge worked like a fiend. First she went to the beauty salon and had her marvelous mane of dark brown hair streaked. Then she had their conventional bedroom done over in— are you braced for this?— mirrors. Smoky mirrors on the walls and ceiling. She packed away the old pink chenille bedspread and replaced it with a huge fake fur throw. The new sheets had a leopard skin design and the lighting was a combination of candle light and those tiny high-intensity reading lamps.

The day that Ted was due back from Pittsburgh Marge called him and said she realized that he would be tired when he got home, but would he please, to humor her, follow exactly the instructions on the notes he would find in the apartment. Ted, his curiosity aroused, agreed.

The first note (on the door) read: "The fact that you're home makes me feel all warm and tingly. Put your suitcase down and go straight to the refrigerator."

The note on the refrigerator said: "Open the door and you will see a very dry martini in a pre-chilled glass. Take your drink to the guest bathroom."

In the bathroom Ted had instructions to soak in the tub of steaming hot water which was awaiting him, while he sipped his martini.

Scotch-taped to the towel he dried himself with was a note that said: "You have the most exciting body I have ever seen. If you want to see for yourself why you are the most sensual man in the world, come to the bedroom."

Ted, thoroughly intrigued (and pretty warm and tingly himself after the bath and martini), walked into the mirrored bedroom, caught sight of Marge stretched out on the fur throw in a black bikini, her body reflected, reflected, reflected everywhere and he flipped out. He never left that bedroom the whole weekend and he let Marge up only long enough to get food and drink occasionally.

Marge doesn't redecorate a room *every* time she feels that Ted could use a little sexual stimulus, but she does come up with the unexpected just often enough to keep him on his toes.

One of the most ingenious ploys I've ever heard of was pulled off by Janet (remember her in Chapter One?), who is so respectable and ladylike in her looks and behavior she would make Emily Post seem like a wanton in comparison.

One Saturday night recently Janet purposely delayed dressing until the very last minute for the dinner party she and her husband were attending. She was so short of time she had to finish applying her make-up in the car and, as they drove up their host's driveway, she was putting on her earrings and gloves. However, Janet stepped from the car bandbox-perfect in her appearance, beautifully groomed and elegantly gowned. She delivered her bombshell as they stood on the steps ringing their host's front bell.

Just as the door started to open and it was too late to retreat, Janet grabbed her husband's arm and gasped, "Oh, Dick, I was in such a hurry, I forgot to put on my panties!"

All evening Dick kept picturing what his very ladylike wife looked like under her proper dress. He wouldn't let another man near her and by the time they started home he had become so excited by Janet's tantalizing and secret nakedness that he couldn't wait to make love to her. They stopped at a motel.

Dick had seen her at six that evening completely naked and nothing had happened to him at all, but the pictures he created in his mind of Janet *partly* naked drove him crazy.

Janet confessed to me the next day that Dick had outdone himself as a lover that night and that she had never felt so wicked and sensual—and desirable.

What are some of the other methods ingenious women have used to fire men's sensuality? One of the wildest I've heard of was a body-painting party, where the six invited couples painted each other's bodies in a rainbow of colors.

A young housewife I know occasionally serves dinner to her husband wearing absolutely nothing above her waist. As a topless hostess she's a great success, for they haven't gotten as far as the dessert course yet.

The simplest way of all to renew your husband's interest is to change your appearance. Just because you have been wearing bangs since you were ten doesn't mean your forehead must be given a life sentence. Try a new style that shows off your high forehead.

If you've been picking out matronly clothes, go buy something youthful and zingy. If you are addicted to drab browns, blacks and greys, change to bright yellow or fire engine red.

If you are pudgy and suddenly take off ten or fifteen pounds, your new svelte figure will be a magnet to him just because it *is* new and unknown.

In the summer when the children are away at camp Sue greets her husband when he comes home at night in exotic costumes and creates a mood to match. One evening she may be a harem girl, the next a Lolita, a Ziegfeld Follies show girl, an eighteenth-century French courtesan, a gypsy fortune teller, a prim schoolteacher who has to be coaxed into unwinding, a Roman slave girl, an Indian maiden.

Ridiculous? Yes and no. Playing glamorous roles makes Sue less irritable over the repetitive household chores that she's stuck with everyday. If while she's scrubbing and waxing the kitchen floor she is also plotting in her mind a geisha girl costume and a beautiful Japanese dinner to go with it, then that floor scrubbing will be done more cheerfully and Jack won't have to deal with a grouchy wife.

She loves getting away from the humdrum and stepping into other worlds. Jack loves being surprised and catered to. You'll never find him lingering at the office to have a drink with the boys. He can hardly wait to get home to

Sue. Jack will never be on the prowl for other women. He has so many at home in the person of Sue that his roving eye is completely satiated.

Now you don't have to match Sue's spectacular productions, but it wouldn't hurt you now and then to greet him after a hard day at the office in your most seductive at-home pajamas, that silly little bikini you didn't quite have the nerve to wear in public or that beautiful peignoir you have packed away in a drawer because it's "too good for everyday wear." Or how about a body stocking or one of his shirts—with nothing on underneath?

If you learn to keep him off guard and curious about what you will be like next, he'll be too focused on you to stray.

Does that mean you can't relax and be yourself? Certainly not. It just means that you should show off all the facets of your personality, not just one or two. You wouldn't wear the same dress every day of your life. Why should you trap yourself into showcasing only one mood or style of living?

It also doesn't mean that you have to be a constant chameleon. Be cozy, lovable old you five days of the week and spring a little glamour and excitement on him the sixth. Not knowing *when* you are going to excite him is part of the fun.

Promise yourself right now to be more inventive in your appearance. I bet you'll learn to enjoy it thoroughly—and he will *love* it.

9.

How to Give to Your Favorite Charity—You

When it was ordained that it was all right and even important for the female to gain sexual satisfaction, the book world found itself riding on a new sales crest. Psychologists, psychiatrists and gynecologists rushed to their typewriters and dictaphones to grind out hundreds of prestige-building and moneymaking marriage manuals advising husbands and wives (single people had to fend for themselves) on

94

what married sex was supposed to be like and how couples should score themselves on sexual satisfaction.

Nearly every modern couple read those books and practiced what the authors preached.

Techniques varied, but the rules were clear. Women were sexually responsive and it was up to the men to arouse and satisfy women, no matter how much effort was involved. Any man, who, through sheer exhaustion or rebellion, chickened out, was a louse.

That old, old rule that woman was designed to give pleasure to man went down the drain when the first marriage manual sale was rung up on the cash register.

The sexual world was now the female's oyster, roles were reversed and we had a clear mandate, after centuries of unexpressed hunger, to feast.

The details of exactly how you should feast depended upon what expert you were reading. The sexual revolution is similar to the revolutions in child care and psychotherapy. Theories and dogma abound and are taken up and discarded like dixie cups.

Women who remained unresponsive were labeled frigid, although only a few years before, that same lack of responsiveness was comfortably touted as normal and even ladylike and not worthy of worry. A great many older women got caught in this trap. It isn't easy to take thirty, forty or fifty years of brainwashing and reverse it suddenly to meet new ideas.

Some of the women who attempted to gain equal opportunity in bed unleashed a Pandora's Box of emasculation wails from husbands who were exposed as inadequate lovers.

There were husbands who got so uptight over the responsibility for and complexity of techniques supposedly necessary to excite their wives that they no longer enjoyed sex, and made love to their wives even less often than before.

Many another husband worked so intensely and humorlessly to arouse his wife that the lady got nervous, felt she *had* to appear passionate when *he was trying so hard* and so faked the erotic feelings she longed to experience.

Some women, afraid to reveal the fact that they were empty sexually, told their husbands and girl friends they were achieving tremendous pleasure and then worried secretly about why they didn't.

The big sexual emancipation, and the flood of conflicting written expert advice that came with it, brought many women large, economy-sized headaches.

By not listening to our instincts, we women made a number of mistakes. This chapter is about our worst mistake, for it cost some of us our men.

We were so busy in bed getting "satisfied" that we forgot our responsibilities as women. We were greedy, selfish and dumb.

We forgot that there were two of us in that bed and that it was just as important to give the man a wonderful experience sexually as it was to receive it.

We forgot what females have been taught since time began: that as women we should be ardent conservationists of our most important natural resource—man—instead of heedlessly using him up.

Pin up on your bed, your mirror, your wall, a sign, lady, until you *know* it in every part of your being: *We were designed to delight, excite and satisfy the male of the species.*

Real women know this.

Don't scream *unfair* to me. Nature is looking out for us, too, for it works both ways: Men were designed to delight, excite and satisfy the female of the species.

The sexes have different ways of going about

it. Men conquer through aggressive and skilled passion and love; women surrender to and are swept up in passion and love.

Now all this is leading to a point I want to make.

If you will go back to Chapter Two, you will notice that the third Key to Sensuality was The Desire To Give.

When you are able to joyfully, tenderly and lustfully offer up every square inch of yourself for him to feast upon and when you are able to use sweetly your erotically skilled body as a sensual instrument to satiate his appetite, then you will find that you will receive a piercingly beautiful pleasure in return. For he will be unable to help rising to the occasion and matching your complete sensuality.

When he is in the company of a master artist (you), he will instinctively seek to reach a similar artistry in his own performance.

I once saw a company of really poor actors turn in performances of high quality when they appeared on the same stage with that great actress (and perfectionist), Judith Anderson. Miss Anderson's inability to accept the mediocre made every actor feel that his life depended upon his being superb and, through sheer force of her presence, the actors released a performance they didn't know was in them. She had to be surrounded by quality and so pulled quality out of them.

This is what you have the power to do to a man in bed. Learn to use it.

No one has more to gain from giving than a woman.

How can you teach yourself to give? You have already made strides. By doing the exercises in Chapters Two and Three you have trained your body to a quicker and more acute response pattern. When your body *feels* more, it automatically gives more because it knows instinctively that by giving of itself it gets. It reaps the dividends of more and better orgasms and more exciting sex. You will know you are successfully giving when your body feels that it is flowing into and with him and that you can't help being swept in any direction he chooses.

A second way of knowing will be his response to your sexual techniques. Chapter Eleven will give you the needed lovemaking skills to induce in him the pleasure he craves.

Remember, the more wonderful you are to him in bed, the more wonderful he will be to you.

Giving can carry you to paradise. A "gimmee,

gimmee" attitude in bed can win you mediocre sex or worse—no sex at all. He's quite likely to dump you for a more responsive partner.

Give—but don't be a Pollyanna, a martyr, a saint or a doormat. Your brain is part of your body, and you must use it.

Learn to be an enlightened giver. If, when you first start to make love to him, he doesn't give back, there are usually two possibilities:

1. He's selfish.
2. He hasn't yet come into full bloom sexually and doesn't know technically and emotionally how to respond completely.

If the bum is selfish, get rid of him. He'll never be worthy of you and you'll be missing a lot of joy with someone else.

If he possesses many good qualities but has a lot to learn sexually—and you like him—help him explore and take command of his sexuality.

Many very sensual men don't come into their prime until their forties or fifties.

One of the most passionate men I have ever known was fifty-six years old before he learned to allow his highly erotic nature to have full rein. All of his life he had kept his sexuality under tight control. In fact, he verged on the puritanical in his sexual attitudes and actions.

When we first made love, my joy in sex and my delight in giving shocked him. I precipitated quite a battle in him, for he disapproved of himself for responding to me and of *me* for being so exciting to him and, worst of all, he couldn't stay away from me. Oh, he did suffer!

I glimpsed the sensuality that was in him and had the patience to wait for it to surface. Within a few weeks he cracked wide open and became an unparalleled lover. Although it took him a while to release it, I never met a man with a heartier sexual appetite and I never met a man who gave more to a woman sexually.

He was worth giving to and waiting for and he's a perfect example of what I mean by enlightened giving.

Don't waste yourself, but don't hold back with a worthwhile man. When you are giving completely to that man, you are giving to your favorite charity—you.

10.

How to Tell in Advance If a Man Will Be a Good Bed Prospect

You may not be able to tell a book by its cover, but you can tell a lot about a man's sexual talents by surface signs.

Without knowing it, he gives you a number of clues to his sensuality.

If you learn to read these clues correctly early in the game, you will get a good idea if he's in your league sexually or if you'd be better off exploring another ball park.

For instance, the eyes can be very revealing—and misleading. Before you allow yourself to be swept away by a pair of brilliant blues or velvety browns, observe how he uses them.

Do his eyes caress and undress your body with obvious pleasure? That's a good sign.

Do you have the feeling he never really looks fully at your body? Even when your back is to him? Watch out. He may be one of those men who are ashamed of the sexual act and who, because of this, give a perfunctory performance.

Does he try to con you with eye games? Penetrating stares that make you feel he can see all the way to your palpitating heart and quivering clitoris, or long soulful looks designed to melt you into mush, are no indications of superior skills. They can be the tools of the second-rate lover.

Are you put off because you're just a haze to him without his glasses? Don't be. Nearsighted men are often marvelous lovers, while there are some male specimens walking around with the vision of an eagle and the sexual prowess of a eunuch.

Is he one of those who don't bother really to focus on your face and individuality while he's making those first sexual overtures? Stay

103

away from him. He isn't interested in *you*, he just wants a convenient bed partner.

Pay attention to his kissing style. If he attacks your mouth with enough force to make you fear he is going to jam your front teeth down your throat, he's going to be even more cloddish in the advanced stages of lovemaking. Unless you are obsessed with medicine, this man is bad news, for you'll be spending half your time with the osteopath getting your shoulder relocated, in the dentist's office getting new teeth, with the bone surgeon getting your delicate fingers set in splints and at the refrigerator getting ice packs for bruises. If, on the other hand, he just pecks at you with dry, pursed lips, he's not likely to make your blood race later. Send him on to some girl who thinks sex is one of the unpleasant duties that come with marriage. They deserve each other.

If he is slobbery, he isn't sensual.

Men who are good lovers invariably use their tongues imaginatively in the early kissing stages. If he uses his tongue badly or not at all, he is going to be equally dull in bed.

When he caresses you, do you tingle and begin to feel warm all over? He's likely to arouse even hotter responses in you when you have your clothes off. However, if he's a blouse crumpler and skirt grabber, he's not going to be any more subtle with your bare skin. Regard him with caution.

Does he treat your breasts like unripe grapefruit instead of firmly but gently caressing them? Who needs him?

Does he keep a lighted cigarette in the ashtray while he's attempting to seduce you? He may be more hooked on tobacco than sex.

Does he arrive for dinner, drink and eat like a pig and then fall asleep on the couch while you are clearing the table? His food hungers may be stronger than his sex drive.

There are many clues to a man's sexual level. If you are alert, you'll catch on to him pretty quickly.

Can he pass all your warning signs and still turn out to be a dud in bed? Yes, you can be completely fooled occasionally. But when you have taught all your senses to tune into the masculine amatory style, you are going to let very few lousy lovers into your life.

Weeding out the clinkers before intimacy is kinder to both of you. You save his male pride from being demolished by knowing what you think of him sexually and you save yourself from a less than happy experience. So, if you are sure he is going to be a terrible bed partner, be merciless and freeze him out of your sexual life. There are too many really marvelous men in this world for you to waste your time on a poor lover just because he's handy or you don't want to go through an ugly scene or hurt his feelings.

11.

How to Drive a Man to Ecstasy

Even the Pilgrims had sex lives. I'm not sure they had *great* sex lives, but they certainly were given to a flurry of activity from time to time. So consider as you are tucking your beautiful body into his bed that you are carrying on a great American tradition—and learn to make love properly.

Proper love today is uninhibited and harmonious love carried out with consummate skill and grace.

Does that mean I'm going to tell you to do some pretty wild things?

Uhmmhmmm. I'm going to tell you *exactly* how to do wild, delicious things to the man you love.

Step by step.

And you, if you have any sense at all, are going to try every single one of them.

What's more, you're going to shock yourself and like a number of these imaginative ways of expressing love and sensuality. For you're becoming a Sensuous Woman now, remember, and it's time to bury forever the idea that there are right and wrong ways to make love.

If you are of the generations that were brought up to believe that sexual intercourse is a woman's unhappy lot, along with menstruation, mounds of laundry and a never-ending pile of dirty dishes, pots and pans, you're going to have to work a little harder than other women to exorcise the ghosts of sexual guilts and bugaboos.

If you are a "freed" daughter of these generations, you too will have to be on your guard, because you absorbed in your childhood that atmosphere of sexual frigidity and, even though you have overcome it through knowledge, occasionally you can be hit by a back-

108

lash. One of those especially vulnerable times is when you are about to try something new sexually. When you feel that icy indictment of a new position or act begin to inhibit you, close your eyes and tell yourself, firmly, that anything that two people lovingly learn to do with each other sexually is decent, respectable and good for you and then go do that something new that you're nervous about *immediately*. You've come too far in your battle to have a healthy, open sexual attitude to let yourself backslide when you come up against the unfamiliar.

In the following sections you will learn the basic moves of the art of love. Some you will like better than others; some *he* will like better than others. *All of them are normal and popular*. Experiment with them, discuss the results with each other and incorporate the things that are most exciting into your lovemaking.

Man's Erogenous Zones

To make love to a man properly you have to know the territory. Most women fail to realize that man's body is absolutely littered with areas that are potential hotbeds of erotic response.

Most men are surprised to find that out, too.

109

They have been so busy concentrating their thoughts and sensations on the penis that they've neglected to discover the rest of themselves.

For instance, did you know that fifty to sixty percent of men have either a partial or full nipple erection? And that some men's breasts may be more erotically responsive than yours?

And did you know that when you bite certain men softly on their buttocks, they get an erection?

And that circling the inside of a man's ear with your tongue can set him all aquiver? And that if you breathe your warm breath into his ear at the same time he might get goose bumps?

And that he may hate it if you play with his belly button?

Each male is a sexual original. Until you have sensually explored every area of your man's body you won't fully know him.

The Head

One of the most erotic areas of a man is the *inside* of his head. His response to sexy pictures, pornographic literature or your voice on the telephone cooing provocative sexual suggestions is usually instantaneous and obvious.

The smart woman never forgets the importance of arousing him mentally. Whispering to him *exactly* what you intend to do to him in bed will create pictures in his mind that are likely to excite him almost as much as the actuality. Reading a provocative scene to him from a spicy book may even pull him away from the eighty-seventh re-run on TV of last week's pro football boners. I say *may* in this case, because if he's a football fan I'm not sure even Sophia Loren could get him away from the TV set when there is pigskin action.

Photographs are amazing. Those crude, tasteless French postcards and magazines may seem crude and tasteless to him too, but while he's looking and saying "how ugly" don't be surprised if he gets the beginning of an erection. You may become all warm and fluttery over a sonnet. Man's temperature rises more quickly with basic literary stimuli. So be sure to keep his mental library well stocked.

The Kiss

The secret of good kissing is a relaxed mouth. *Never, never* pucker your lips, or kiss

111

with the lips and teeth sealed firmly shut. How would *you* like to kiss someone who feels like he's in the early stages of lockjaw? Well, he won't like it either. Let your lips go almost limp. Ease the tension from your chin. Automatically your teeth will part slightly and you will be able to slip that teasing tongue of yours into his mouth as the pressure of the kiss (and your passion) mounts.

Naturally you will follow his lead while kissing, but there is a great deal you can do that he can't regard as "taking over." The trick is to slip in an embellishment here and there of your own in response to him. For instance, when you are coming up for air after one of those long, hungry soul kisses, lightly and quickly kiss him on the eyes, the nose, the forehead, hair, chin and then the mouth again, pulling the right side of his upper lip into your mouth and then the whole lower lip with a gentle sucking motion, releasing and then running your tongue silkily across his front teeth, gums and around and down inside his lips and then let yourself be swept into a deep kiss again. Uhmmm. How delicious.

Remember those tongue exercises in Chapter Two? See how that increased flexibility aids you in probing deep into his mouth, in

112

darting under, over and around his tongue? Notice your new strength as you suction his tongue into your mouth? And the thrill he gets when you run that tongue of yours lingeringly across his cheek, down his neck, across his chest to his left breast? Run your tongue around the nipple a few times, then across his chest to the other nipple, excite it and then back up to his mouth. No man could stay indifferent with a mouth like yours tantalizing him.

Kiss him everywhere and return again and again to the places he likes most.

Pelvic and Vaginal Muscles and the Amazing Sensations They Can Create

When I get sexually aroused my body just *has* to wriggle. I've always been that way. For several years I thought it was an affliction, and on dates I used to concentrate so hard to suppress that revealing wriggle that I wasn't able to enjoy fully the kissing. I had been brought up properly and there was no doubt in my mind: No nice girl wriggled.

You can only be that stupid when you are young, I suppose.

In later years when I let my body go its own natural way, I was dumbfounded to discover that my shameful pelvic wriggle was the object of much admiration in the opposite sex. It was sensuous. And men became fascinated with the desire to find out how their penis would feel imbedded in the center of that rhythmic and provocative wriggle. One man confessed to me that for several months he had a re-occurring sexual dream along those lines.

Men are always hypnotized by undulating movements. There is nothing more hypnotic than a belly dancer, and the stripper's repertoire of bumps and grinds, even when performed in dead-face boredom, still fascinates the audience.

Learn to move your pelvis and behind as if they were loaded with ball bearings. Lie on your back, weight resting on your shoulders and arms, lift your hips off the bed a few inches and make imaginary designs with that part of your body. First try circles, clockwise and counterclockwise, then do a figure eight and a square. Now let your buttock muscles push your pelvic area up and back down again, up and down, up and down. Think of what his penis would feel like deep within you as you move. Uhmhmm. Very nice. And think of the sensations you are giving *him*. Now suck in your vaginal muscles as if you were trying to imprison his penis. Relax, constrict the muscles again and relax again. If you have been doing Sensuality Exercise Number 7 (the Bonnie Prudden sexercises), you'll be able to carry off a dozen different gripping and thrusting actions with practically no effort.

If you have been malingering, get at it. When a man enters a woman, she's not supposed to lie there like a rag doll, she's supposed to meet and become enmeshed in his thrusts, entice his penis to throb and hunger for the depths of her and make him feel that the center of the universe is her pulsating and maddening vagina.

That takes muscle.

What do you get out of it? Three things:

1. The knowledge that you're driving him wild sexually.
2. These exercises are most helpful in slimming the waist and hips, flattening the tummy and tightening the derrière.
3. Your increased flexibility allows you to tilt your pelvis to get maximum clitoral stimulation, and we both know the positive results of that!

So start working on those gluteals, abdominals and levator. The Sensuous Woman (that's you, remember) also has to be superb at—

Nibbling, Nipping, Eating, Licking and Sucking

Now don't turn up your nose and make that ugly face! Oral sex is, for most people who will give it a real try, delicious. It is part of the Sensuous Woman's bag of pleasures and has the added advantage, if you're a snob, of being a status style of lovemaking. (It's the preferred way with many movie stars, artists, titled Europeans and jet setters.)

Does the idea of putting a man's penis in your mouth revolt you? If so, you are probably a typical product of America's taboos against oral gratification. After all, we've been trained to think that one of the most natural and beautiful acts in the world, that of a mother nursing her child, is embarrassing and offensive to the eye. Why shouldn't we believe that it's unsanitary and wrong to put our lips to an area of the body that's been in our vagina and is used regularly to urinate?

Actually, kissing a man's penis is a lot less unsanitary than kissing him on the mouth. The mouth and throat are real hotbeds of germs.

For that matter, you're going to be exposed to more infections and diseases at a PTA meeting than in bed. As for oral-genital sex being wrong, realize that the only thing wrong with it is that *you think* it's wrong.

The first time a man "went down on me" (officially called cunnilingus when he does it to you and fellation when you do it to him— actually, both sexes usually skip the scientific terms and say eating), I was, frankly, a little shocked. I couldn't imagine why he would want to do such a distasteful thing. Although I kept quiet, my feelings must have communicated themselves to him, for he quickly retreated (much to my relief!) and returned to the "correct" way of making love: coitus, with the man on top and the woman on the bottom and all kissing limited to mouth to mouth.

As I became more involved in lovemaking, I discovered that, not only was it apparently normal for a man to desire oral-genital contact with a woman, he almost invariably wanted her (who, me?!?) to reciprocate.

All of my puritanical upbringing resisted this idea. However, the practical side of me pointed out that, while I might be unenthusiastic about oral sex, I was *very* enthusiastic about coitus and a few minutes of oral-genital

117

play was a small price to pay for the great pleasure I derived from the rest of lovemaking.

So I decided it was in my own best interests to keep my mouth open (in this case) and learn a few basic oral techniques to please and excite the man I loved.

After a while, through sheer repetition, I managed to overcome my revulsion. I wasn't gung-ho on oral sex, but I didn't mind it and I did achieve some pleasure emotionally from making my partner happy.

It never occurred to me that I would ever find oral sex fulfilling, but thanks to an explosive experience with a wildly uninhibited man from Chicago, I finally tuned in to the joys of oral gratification.

The evening of my enlightenment began at New York's posh Pavillon Restaurant and ended two days later when we emerged, drained and serene, from his Manhattan penthouse. During those forty-eight hours, that wonderful man transmitted to me his own ecstatic delight in all things oral by, first, using superlative oral and manipulative techniques steadily for long periods of time to keep me at a pitch of arousal where it was almost impossible for me not to respond in kind and, two, by his completely taking for granted that I was as enthusiastic as he was about every aspect of sex. As it turned out, he was right. Suddenly, in that adventurously free atmosphere all those muscles of mine that had been secretly resisting, reversed themselves, pushing out, desiring and craving. My mouth and tongue were hungry to taste and feel all of him. So I did. Wow! It was even better than caviar and champagne, both of which, come to think of it, I had disliked on first sampling. Obviously it takes my taste buds a while to catch on to the good things of life.

You may never learn to love oral sex, but there are two excellent reasons for you to become at least an adequate performer:

1. Experimentation will probably ease inhibitions and increase your and your mate's mutual sense of intimacy.
2. Your man will love you for it.

Here are some basic oral techniques:

P/M—PENIS/MOUTH TECHNIQUE

Have the man lie on his back. Kneel at the right or left side of him so that your knees are at right angles to his hip. Bend over and take the penis and place it gently in the palm of your hand. Run your tongue around the head

119

so that it is thoroughly moistened and then wet your lips with your tongue. Now stretch your mouth until it covers the tops of both rows of your teeth. There are two reasons for this. One, you must avoid inadvertently nicking or cutting the very tender skin of the penis; and, two, the covered teeth form a firm, smooth ridge that is very effective in creating sensation in this highly responsive organ.

When you have formed the ridge, take the penis and insert it into your mouth. Slowly move your mouth down to the base of the penis, and then back up to the head again. If you don't have enough lubrication to slide the penis in and out of your mouth easily, re-wet it a few times with your tongue. By experimenting, you will discover what speed of manipulation your man prefers. He may like you to stick to a slow, steady in-and-out stroke, or prefer a strong, quick stroke or maybe a combination of both.

After you have mastered the P/M, add the Butterfly Flick and the Silken Swirl to that basic technique.

THE BUTTERFLY FLICK

One of the most arousing things you can do to a man is the Butterfly Flick. On the under-

side of the penis, about one to two inches behind the head, is a ridge called the corona.
Just underneath the corona is a delicate verti-
cal membrane. This is the most sensitive area
of the man's body. To drive him straight to
ecstasy, take your tongue and flick it *lightly*
back and forth across this membrane—like
you were strumming a banjo. Now run your
tongue down to the base of the penis and back
up again a few times and then return to the
Butterfly Flick, only this time flicking all the
way up and down the underside of the penis.
Continue until the man begs for mercy.

THE SILKEN SWIRL

This is really sensuous. In the Silken Swirl
you continually circle the penis clockwise or
counterclockwise with your tongue as you are
sliding the penis in and out of your mouth. You
may find it a bit hard to coordinate both actions at first, but practice, for the effect the
Silken Swirl has on the male makes it well
worth the effort.

THE HOOVER

Some men are very fond of the Hoover, especially if they haven't yet attained a full erection. In this one you use your mouth like a tiny

vacuum cleaner, sucking the penis into your mouth until it is inserted about half way; then, still exerting the vacuum pressure, slowly start to slide the penis from your mouth. This double pulling action can be very exciting.

GNAWING

There is an occasional man who likes you to gnaw or chew on his penis, but be extremely careful in experimenting with this, as one false bite will put him out of action for weeks. Rough handling here may also give him a slightly negative attitude toward you as a future bed partner. Of course, if you're tired of him, this is an excellent way to discourage further advances.

THE WHIPPED CREAM WRIGGLE

If you have a sweet tooth, this is the one for you. Take some freshly whipped cream, to which you have added a dash of vanilla and a couple of teaspoons of powdered sugar and spread the concoction evenly on the penis so that the whole area is covered with a quarter-inch layer of cream. As a finishing touch, sprinkle on a little shredded coconut and/or chocolate. Then lap it all up with your tongue. He'll wriggle with delight and you'll have the fun of an extra dessert. If you have a weight problem, use one of the many artificial whipped creams now on the market (available in boxes, plastic containers and aerosol cans) and forego the coconut and chocolate.

POSITIONS

There are an endless number of good positions in which to engage in oral-genital sex. If you can find it, read *Oralgenitalism—An Encyclopaedic Outline of Oral Technique in Genital Excitation* by Roger-Maxe de la Glannege (Gershon Legman). Legman says there are as many as 14,288,400 positions in cunnilingus! That ought to keep the average couple busy a while.

The most famous position is Sixty-Nine, where you surmount the man in a face-to-face position, but facing in opposite directions (are you still with me?), so that while you are caressing his genitals, he can caress yours. You don't always have to stay on top. Being on the bottom is pretty interesting too.

You can try lying side by side; he can lie flat while you kneel between his legs; you can sit on the floor while he leans back so that his genitals are on the edge of a bed, table or chair; he can stand while you nibble from below

123

(tricky for you if you're making it in a swimming pool, but not impossible). All these positions are effective. Try them and go on to invent a few new ones.

Keep in mind (and tongue) that there is a great deal more to a man than his penis. While you're working away in that area, move downward with your tongue to his balls (testicles). Lightly lick the balls all over and then try something that a number of men find very exciting. Take a testicle and slide it into your mouth. But be very, very gentle. You will cause him excruciating pain if you are rough. Think of his testicle as an egg and be extremely careful not to crack that shell!

Now just behind the testicles and in front of the anus is a sensitive little patch that is also responsive to the tongue. Be sure not to overlook it in your oral wanderings. The Butterfly Flick is nice here.

Other places that men love to be licked are the inside of the thighs, the belly button, the nipples of the breasts, the back of the neck, the ears and, well, actually, *everywhere.*

NIPPING AND NIBBLING

Men also like it when you nibble (light, affectionate biting) on such places as the ear

124

lobes, lips, breasts, buttocks and toes. Nipping (sharper biting) is less popular, but does have its aficionados. If he goes crazy over the nibbling, slip in a nip or two and see if he reacts favorably.

All of this stimulation of the man is going to bring him close to orgasm, which is a compliment to the art of sensuality you are learning to practice so well. Learn to bring him up to that point of climax and then slow down again several times. Then when he finally does come, it should be a more intense orgasm.

When your man reaches that final peak, he could decide to come in your mouth. Did I shock you again? Yes, this is another completely normal sex act. Men in the main seem to get a bigger kick out of this than women. Of the females I surveyed (all pretty uninhibited according to their mates) about one-third enjoyed it and two-thirds didn't. Apparently when it comes to this, a lot of pretty sensuous women desert the ship, or would like to. Oh no you don't! No skipping out for you! I bet you never even tried it. Don't say, "This isn't for me." You don't know yet. Make a fairly long-term effort to feel the pleasure in this highly sensual adventure.

Mouth/penis orgasm gives you the opportunity to *really* feel and share the explosion of his coming to climax (you just don't have the sensitivity in the vagina) and this can be a thrilling experience for a woman. If you'd like an added bonus, remember it's also pretty hard to get pregnant this way.

This Is No Time
to Sit on Your Hands

Oh, those lovely hands of yours. How they can excite. Unfortunately, most women are lazy and unimaginative in the use of their hands as sexual instruments. You are not going to ruin your new manicure or overtax any muscles by letting him know directly that he's so sexy you can't keep your hands off him.

Never, never let your hands be idle during lovemaking. There is always some area of his body you can reach to set on fire with your touch. When you are on your back and he is on top of you, you can run your fingers up and down his back, across his buttocks, over the anus, up the sides of the torso to the back of his neck and then along the shoulders and down the center of his spinal column and still continue primary intercourse. If you are on top of him you can caress his chest and arms. If you

126

are in the Sixty-Nine position, you can stroke his buttocks and legs.

You went to a lot of trouble in Sensuality Exercises 1, 2 and 3 to learn tactile awareness and skill. Now use your knowledge to excite, soothe and know him more intimately.

You can drive him wild by artfully handling his genitals.

You can relax him by giving him a good massage.

Exploring every part of his body with loving hands will increase your sense of intimacy. Memorize all the variations of skin texture, from the roughness of his legs to the miraculously velvety feel of the head of the penis. Get to know that funny little bump on his left shoulder blade, run your fingers through the hair on his chest, feel the muscles in his arms expand and contract, and the toughness of his feet, the delicacy of his eyelids. There is so much of him to discover. After a while you should be able to pick out your man blindfolded by using your tactile memory.

If you've been sitting on your hands, get up off your pretty behind and start giving them a workout. Your hands are important lovemaking instruments and, used artistically, they are a unique sexual signature.

Anal Sex

I know it seems as if I never stop telling you about shocking sex acts. Well, cheer up. This is an optional. No one's going to call you square and you are no less a woman if you say no to anal sex after trying it. There are some good reasons for *not* doing this one.

There are also a number of good reasons *for* doing it.

When I first heard about anal sex, it sounded evil and dirty and sick to me. The thought that nice people might engage in anal activity never entered my mind but, if it had, I'm sure I would have pictured an outraged God rising up and punishing the perverts by giving them leprosy or, at the very least, hemorrhoids.

But nice people are copulating anally every day of the week and nothing horrible or even unpleasant happens to them.

In an extended relationship with a man, the idea of trying anal caressing and manipulation and rectal intercourse almost invariably is discussed. The male's search for new sexual experiences usually makes him the initiator of anal advances.

First he may wish to investigate you anally

128

with his mouth and tongue and expect you to reciprocate. Now don't freeze. If you have washed in this area, it is *not* dirty and, if you'll stop wailing like a banshee or playing Purity Raped for a moment, you will notice the beginning of a curious, warm and divinely demanding sensation and be secretly hoping he'll go on to the next step in anilingus, which is the entry of a well-lubricated finger into the anus followed by manipulation of the finger in an in-and-out motion and maybe a circular motion. Again, this is a reciprocal act.

For rectal intercourse (you're not going to chicken out at this point, are you?) the most comfortable position is for you to lie on your stomach with your hips elevated by one or two pillows. Your partner will apply surgical jelly or vaseline generously to his penis and your anus and then *slowly* and *gently* enter you fully. If he doesn't treat you like the fragile creature you are in this area, don't just speak up—shout. Most men, however, are very sensitive to the possibility of causing you discomfort if they are too abrupt in their movements and are extremely careful.

After he has entered you completely, the man will slowly begin an in-and-out stroke and treat your anus as if it was your vagina.

Once you have let your sphincter muscle relax, you will find yourself enjoying some quite remarkable sensations and, if you encourage your partner to play with your clitoris while he is making anal love to you, you are capable of having quite an orgasm.

He may choose to come to climax at this time or withdraw and finish the lovemaking vaginally. Either way is very nice.

The bad features of anal lovemaking are:

1. Your mental attitude. If you have been brought up to think that this act is degenerate and dirty, it will initially be hard for you to enjoy thoroughly the delights of anal sex.

2. Unless you both are squeaky clean, it can be most distasteful. If you suspect your bedmate's most recent brush with soap and water was in honor of his graduation from high school, you can always suggest taking a sexy bubble bath or shower together before lovemaking. When he understands that his cleanup includes some loving caresses on his private parts, you shouldn't have any trouble leading him to water regularly.

3. If, after withdrawing from your anus, he fails to wash his penis before entering your vagina, you can get vaginitis.

4. Some women who fail to relax tense muscles

fully, find that the anal area is tender and even sore after anal intercourse. Increased experience and enthusiasm should alleviate this problem.

The good features of anal lovemaking are:

1. It adds variety to lovemaking.
2. You can't get pregnant, so if you've forgotten to take your pills or you're caught without your diaphragm, you are not limited to oral sex.
3. If you are having an especially heavy menstrual period and feel that vaginal intercourse would be too messy, this is an effective sexual alternative.
4. This is the really important one: Anal sex opens up to you a whole new area of pleasurable sensations to be relished by you and used to increase your personal sexual satisfaction.

Now what's bad about that?

The Thing That Turns Him on You Think Is Sick

If he wants to resort to whips and chains or have you urinate on him or something of that nature, I agree with you, I think he's sick—and he should let you alone and go find a simpatico sickie or, better yet, get professional help.

131

Or, if he insists upon practicing one sexual act like fellation, cunnilingus or rectal intercourse to the exclusion of all others, I think that's sick too. And dull.

But if he tries to inveigle you into making love with your nylons and shoes on occasionally, likes to lick honey from your vagina every few weeks, gets a more powerful orgasm if you whisper earthy words in his ear, prefers sex with all the lights blazing away or wants to try every position known to man, he can't be labeled sick or even far out.

Unless you have an ultra-strong aversion to his pet sexual practice, be a good sport and make it pleasurable for him. In return he is likely to be generous in doing what you like best sexually.

The surprising thing about an offbeat sexual practice is that, after it has been a regular part of your lovemaking for a while, you may find yourself responding to it. Familiarity does not necessarily breed contempt. It sometimes breeds mutual pleasure and contentment.

But let's suppose that after trying his pet sexual kick for a while you really feel you can't endure it. Then tell him so frankly and suggest some new and titillating lovemaking ideas that you both might enjoy equally and ask him to think of some adventurous alternative sexual practices that you two can experiment with. Chances are, if you honestly are trying and not just copping out as a woman and as a good bed partner, that you will quickly find a happy substitute and your sex life will be zooming again.

It is not unusual for us to be wary or even afraid of new and different sexual practices. But it is wrong to let our trepidations deprive us of the fun of sexual variety and it is also wrong of us to deprive our mates of harmless sexual larks that give them pleasure.

So, before you label your lover "sick," consider the possibility that he could label you "narrow and prudish."

12.

Aphrodisiacs

I made the mistake of reading up on so-called aphrodisiacs, or love potions, after eating a hearty lunch. Ugh. The potions that gullible people have downed in an attempt to increase sexual prowess would turn any but the strongest stomachs. Like, how does a tasty dish of mashed-up alligators and lizards stir your innards? Or perhaps you would prefer a concoction of dead bees tossed in a bottle with a little liquid, sealed, left to disintegrate for a couple of months—and then shaken well and swallowed. Or would you be tempted by a serving of powdered partridge brains? If I had to drink those mixtures I would be crawling into a sick bed instead of a love bed. Most of the world must agree with me, for these ancient brews have fallen out of favor.

Not all of the aphrodisiacs that men and women have taken over the centuries have been revolting. Some, such as special creams and oils, you didn't have to eat at all, you just rubbed them on the appropriate organ. They didn't stir the sexual juices, but they did give you good skin texture.

Other aphrodisiacs have been downright delectable, like oysters, artichokes, caviar, honey, chocolate, eggs, avocados, asparagus, raw (or rare) beef, mushrooms, truffles and lobster.

Delicious foods, yes. Aphrodisiacs, no. Those legends about the magic properties of various foods are all a lot of bunk, I'm sorry to say; and, while I'm disillusioning you, I might as well add a few more categories to the nonaphrodisiac list, like roots, herbs and vitamins.

There are a surprising number of people who really believe that ginseng (instant or regular), damiana, aposte, myrtle and burdock will make you sexier. I'm afraid if it does it's a purely psychological response, as none of these roots and herbs has the power to stir you physically.

Now about vitamins and sex.

The great vitamin controversy rages on. While there has been research done with cattle showing that vitamin E helps bulls to be better breeders, there is no proof that the bull enjoys it more and there has been no definitive research at all on the possibility that vitamin E can help people achieve increased sexual stimulation. Go ahead and try 100 International Units a day if you wish. It won't harm you and, if you get any results, let me know. Hordes of people began taking vitamin E a couple of years ago when a magazine article touted it as a sexual stimulant. Of the people I personally knew (including myself) who went on the vitamin E jag, not one reported any increased sexuality.

I asked a nutritionist and several doctors about the rumor that para-aminobenzoic acid (called PABA, for obvious reasons) is an aphrodisiac. The doctors all pooh-poohed it, although they admitted they hadn't tried this little-known B vitamin. The nutritionist wouldn't say if he had used PABA as an aphrodisiac or not, but he did state that while PABA didn't work for women there was a *possibility* that, taken in the right dosages, PABA might have an aphrodisiac effect on men. But before you get too interested, remember that no laboratory or field tests have been run to prove or disprove it and some nutritionists feel that PABA, taken in large amounts, can cause a deficiency of other B vitamins.

Vitamin C is supposed to give rabbits increased sexual stamina, but there, again, there is no evidence that Vitamin C is anything more than a necessary booster of good health in the human.

I am discouraging, aren't I?

Here are a few more. Pomegranates, ambergris, poppy seeds and nutmeg will not turn you on sexually, and I guess by now *everyone* knows that Spanish Fly is *not* an aphrodisiac but a horrible drug that can cause torturous sensations in the female and even kill her.

There is only one aphrodisiac in this world, and that is love.

No chemistry lab will ever be able to duplicate the wondrous effect his look, his voice and his caress have on your body.

So forget about science or witchcraft coming up with a wonder mix that will set your glands on fire and concentrate on teaching your body to respond naturally. Once you have trained yourself to be a Sensuous Woman, you won't need any artificial stimulants.

However, we have learned a few things from the endless experiments of the aphrodisiac hounds that you should keep in mind. For instance, alcohol, taken in small quantities, can be an effective relaxing agent for a man who is still tense and mentally reliving a rough business day. And the wise woman now knows to feed a man a high protein and low carbohydrate dinner if she wants a good sexual performance from him that night. If she stuffs him with macaroni, bread, potatoes, rich sauces and cake at seven he'll be snoring in front of the TV set by nine and maybe dead with a coronary by ten. Most of the so-called aphrodisiacs in the food category, like oysters, asparagus, mushrooms and lobster are high-energy, low-calorie foods. If you pop them into his gullet for dinner he's not going to turn into a sex fiend, but after a stack of oysters he'll still have room and appetite for you.

Another effective love inducer for the tired, draggy man is sleep. When he staggers in from work, make him take a hot bath, give him a gentle massage and then let him sleep for half an hour. When he wakes up he'll be ready to handle you most improperly.

But the best way of all to keep your sex life at aphrodisiac level is to find a man worth loving, who feels the same way about you, and then guard and work hard to deepen the love you feel for each other.

So become a Sensuous Woman and you'll never find yourself desperately swallowing a dose of mashed lizards or decomposed bees to make you feel sexy. He'll be able to make you feel that way just by touching you.

13.

Sex—Where to Have It

Many of the men who wander do so to satisfy a craving for adventure. To keep these men coming home to you, you must be sure that your lovemaking contains a variety of techniques (if I am becoming a bit of a nag about that, it's only because it's so important) and you *must* every now and then introduce a note of daring into your sexual relationship.

What do I mean by daring? Offbeat or at

least different locations—like on the living room rug, on or under the dining room table (no, I haven't gone completely whacky), in the bathtub, on a deserted beach, in the woods. There are hundreds of unusual spots.

If you think there is only one place to make love—in bed—then it's time to broaden your horizons. I'm not suggesting you give up the comfort of the bedroom regularly. Only that you vary your lovemaking locations at unexpected intervals. Unusual surroundings excite most men, and you have everything to gain and nothing to lose by being imaginative enough to keep the shadow of boredom from falling across your lovemaking.

I follow my own advice. I've made love in an Eames chair (so-so), in a four-seater plane one mile up in the air (an uplifting and slightly giddy feeling), on top a marble coffee table (sexy), by moonlight on the green of the twelfth hole of a golf course (very romantic, and that special grass they grow for greens felt wonderful on my bare skin!), under a bed (I'll never do that again), on the deserted stage of a theatre (stimulated me to reach a very high performance level), in a swimming pool (all right, but not great and it's a pretty run of the mill spot nowadays, I'm told) and other places that don't come to mind immediately.

Did I lose *his* respect by being so wild? Hardly. He treats me like a rare and precious jewel and he goes around proud of the fact that with me he is the world's most imaginative lover.

Now I'm not an exhibitionist or contortionist and I like big, soft beds for lovemaking. But the man I love craves the unexpected and unknown every now and then and I'll be darned if I'm going to, through lack of energy and imagination, encourage him to find that new experience with some sexy young thing at the office. He's a fantastic man and worth swinging from a chandelier for occasionally.

Remember Grace, that gorgeous wife I told you about in Chapter One, who had the wandering husband? She got his complete attention again when one rainy Sunday afternoon she enticed him to make love to her on their pool table (luckily a sturdy model). That proved so successful that a few nights later she led him naked into their dark back yard, where the possibility of discovery turned Bill into a honeymoon-type lover again. Grace varies her surprises. Sometimes she wears sexy costumes, sometimes she'll select an unusual place or time of day to suggest to Bill. Last month, for instance, Grace prepared a delicious picnic lunch for Bill and took it to his office. They locked his office door, closed the blinds and between nibbles of caviar and pungent cheeses, they nibbled on each other.

Bill is in ecstasy over the new Grace and she admitted to me that, once she got into the spirit of things, she got unbelievably excited herself. Her biggest surprise was psychological: She realized that she didn't feel one bit less lady-like on that pool table than she did playing baseball with the kids. Grace had always assumed that women who allowed themselves to become erotic weren't very "nice." Now she knows that in continuing that tired old cliché of female thinking she was only cheating herself.

Again, let me stress that Grace doesn't create these sexual diversions steadily. Only when she feels Bill's desire needs a stimulus or if she herself thinks of something crazy that she feels like experimenting with. Needless to say, when Bill suggests an unusual spot to make love, Grace doesn't put on a long-suffering face, she cooperates with zest.

More men than you would believe thrive on that slight sense of danger. The threat of discovery sets their blood racing. A well-known playboy confessed to me that the most exciting sexual experience he ever had was when he made love to the wife of a banker while the banker was sleeping in the twin bed next to them!

Men pick amazing places for sexual adventures. Some of the more trustworthy gentlemen I interviewed acknowledged that they had had intercourse in—are you ready for these?—the Tomb of the Unknown Soldier, New York's Philharmonic Hall the week it opened, the cupola of our nation's Capitol, a BOAC London-to-New-York flight (first class, of course) and the private elevator of the president of a major TV network.

Other less reliable men *said* they had made love in the Huntington Hartford Museum, the ladies' room of the Harvard Club, the choir loft of a church (I heard several variations on that one), underneath the bleachers at a rodeo, in a balloon (he actually did know a balloonist, so maybe he was telling the truth), a bandshell in a park on a rainy day and a department store window (the shades were closed) at night while the window was being decorated.

The most outlandish story I heard came from an unimpeachable source. It seems that during World War II, Captain Robert ——, age twenty-seven, was a fighter pilot with the 57th Flight Group stationed at Grosetto Airport in the Po Valley, Italy. One day he took an attractive nurse up with him in his tiny plane and there they were, tooting along at 6,500 feet, the Germans shooting away at them with 40-millimeter and 88-millimeter anti-aircraft fire. And what were Captain Robert and the nurse doing while their plane was being riddled? You're right. Making love. I'd never be that brave—or insane. I'm afraid to ride on a Ferris wheel, much less go up in a plane that's guaranteed to attract a bunch of trigger-happy Germans.

But the male animal seems to thrive on such nuttiness.

The wildest sex adventure that appealed to *me*, and I have to admit that I haven't tried it yet, is in Ruth Dickson's book *Married Men Make the Best Lovers*. Miss Dickson suggests making love in a bathtub filled with Jello! I wonder how many boxes it would take? What would be the most alluring color and flavor? If the Jello gets firm, would you bounce and, if so, how high? And what happens to the drains when you rinse that melted Jello out of your tub?

You, if you will look around and allow your

145

imagination to operate, will find a number of different and, yes, even *romantic* places to make love. How about that patch of clover near your mountain cabin? Or the float at the lake, late some hot summer night when no one is around? Or the guest bedroom? The leather couch in his den? The recreation room? A sailboat? In front of a crackling fire?

There are so many quite wholesome places for you to try that offer an air of mystery—because they are unknown to you as *lovemaking* settings.

Try two or three. I think you'll be surprised at the special sparkle that will be added to your lovemaking when you break with routine.

Remember those three important weapons that you should learn to wield effectively if you are going to keep the man you love in love with you:

1. Imagination.
2. Sensitivity to his moods and desires.
3. The courage to experiment with new sexual techniques, enticing situations and places.

If you want a loving, exciting man, you can't afford to loll around the house in an "I'm perfect just as I am, I don't have to make any effort to please him" attitude. If he's a first-rate man, some other woman is going to steal him from you and we both know the dire results of that: You can't be an actively sensuous woman without a man!

14.

What to Talk About in Bed and When to Laugh

Women are more romantic than men in their bed talk. If ever there is a time when a man is *less* inclined toward whispering sweet nothings into the ear of his heart's delight, it's while he is in the middle of making love to her.

Before or after lovemaking he will dash off sonnets and deluge her with verbal bouquets, but not during.

And yet it's during lovemaking that women

want most to hear detailed and embroidered "I love you's."

There is definitely a communications gap between the sexes when they climb into bed, and it is the woman who is expected to bridge that gap.

How? By learning the language of sex. Lovemaking is physical and so is the language that so aptly describes it.

Fuck, suck, box, cunt, cock and prick are not bad words when used in context. Scrawled on a wall they are dirty words, but used in the bedroom by lovers to describe parts of the body and physical activities, they are very proper usage and they distinctly enhance sexual activity. Whispering "I love you" to the average man doesn't have nearly the exciting effect on him that "your cock makes me so hot I can hardly stand it" does.

If you've been bristling every time your man uses a four-letter word while making love to you, start overhauling your prudish attitude. He is not being vulgar, nor will you be by talking his language in bed. After you have used a few of the "forbidden" sex words, you will realize how "correct" they are—and how sexy.

Four-letter words are not all you should murmur in bed. Man's ego is very fragile and before, during and just after lovemaking are prime times to bolster that ego with compliments. If you've gotten as far as the bedroom with him he must have *some* attributes that you can extol. His brawny chest, maybe, or magnetic eyes or sexy buttocks. Try to develop a sense of wonder at his personal construction. Adonis? No. Cary Grant? No. But still uniquely beautiful in his originality. Verbalize your discoveries.

But don't lie. If he has a small penis and you tell him that it's the biggest one in the world, he's not going to believe you. Instead, mention the fact that it tastes so good and feels so good in you (assuming it does). You've told the truth and pleased him enormously.

Praise his sexual prowess. Even great lovers need to have their talents reaffirmed, and your man is not immune to being told how terrific he is. Your admiration will probably spur him on to even greater sexual heights, and there's nothing wrong with that!

Take your sense of humor to bed with you. Richard Burton said something I agree with in a recent magazine interview:

> If you can't laugh together in bed, the chances are you are incompatible, anyway. I'd rather hear a girl laugh well than try to turn me

on with long, silent, soulful, secret looks. If you can laugh with a woman, everything else falls into place.

The bedroom is also a good location for you both to talk to each other without inhibition about worries and dreams. The special intimate and relaxed atmosphere following lovemaking is an ideal time to coax him into opening up to you verbally.

15.

Men's Fantasies

Whew! Did I have a hard time getting men to talk about this one! They voluntarily and even eagerly, in some cases, confided to me their most intimate sexual experiences, but the minute I would move on to the subject of sexual fantasies, men clammed up. A good proportion denied ever having any, and even those that admitted that they did indulge in a fantasy or two now and then, when asked to recount the fantasy, suddenly had amnesia.

So for a complete study of what men conjure up in their minds to stimulate themselves sexually when they daydream, masturbate or make love, you will have to consult the professional literature. The only male fantasies I was able to pry out of eight reluctant volunteers were these:

Fantasy Number One

You're not going to like this one at all! While he's making love to you he imagines you are Brigitte Bardot, a young Rita Hayworth, Audrey Hepburn, Ava Gardner, your next-door neighbor or whoever else visually makes him flip sexually.

Fantasy Number Two

A gorgeous unknown female is chained to the wall. He begins to do very erotic things to her while she writhes in helpless resistance. Slowly, thanks to his superb technique (it's his fantasy, after all, and he would naturally be a remarkable lover), she begins to respond to him and then goes crazy with passion. Slowly he unchains her and she throws herself upon him and makes love to *him.*

153

Fantasy Number Three

This one is as common as rhododendron. At least two and sometimes three, four, five or even six women of various hues and shapes all make love to the fantasizer at once. Sometimes this takes place at an orgy. Other times they are alone.

Fantasy Number Four

He lies there helpless to resist while this enchanting vision of female sexuality forces herself upon him, finally completely possessing him.

Fantasy Number Five

Remember that famous old line, "I suppose you wonder why I brought you all together here today"? Not all sexual fantasies include the sex act. One man told me he enjoyed imagining a beautiful party in an elegant room and he, as the host, silently relishing the fact that he has at one time or another made love to every female in the room. Naturally it's a big party.

154

Fantasy Number Six

The fantasizer enters a building with many rooms. In each room is a female, each one entirely original in physical appearance, age and sexual proclivities and he goes from room to room satisfying each woman in a different way.

I know I said I got eight men to talk and I only told you six fantasies, but three of them described Fantasy Number 3 to me. The eight men were divided on the question of whether they would like their fantasies to come true. Five were all for a real life reenactment of their dreams, three said it would spoil it for them—that the whole point of a fantasy was that it *was* a fantasy.

If you can coerce your man into revealing his secret sexual imagery to you, bravo. Not only is it extremely interesting, it will also be helpful to you to know what goes on in his head sexually. If he's one of those men who would like to act out his fantasy and you feel it would be fun to do so, just think what a thrill you may be able to give him. Too, if you've been longing to bring a fantasy of your own to life he can hardly refuse to cooperate when you have been so delightful to him.

16.

Party Sex—Swapping and Orgies and Why It's Better Sometimes to Bring Your Own Grapes

A funny thing has been going on for the last few years in America. Canasta, mah-jongg, poker, bali, bridge and bingo are getting serious competition from the country's newest game—the orgy.

Respectable couples are actually going to parties, taking off all their clothes and having intercourse with as many of the other guests as their stamina will allow—and all in full view of each other.

It's not exactly what the marriage counselors had in mind when they suggested that a couple share a hobby they both would enjoy once a week that gets them out of the house, but ardent orgiasts swear that sex parties are one of the main keys to a happy marriage.

Orgies accomplish this feat by allowing tired and bored sex partners to be recharged in controlled circumstances (guests and locations are carefully screened) and openly. Since your mate is with you, you can hardly be accused of deceit.

Instead of sneaking around and having an affair on the side that because of its emotional involvement can endanger the marriage, orgiasts say that the impersonal climate of an orgy precludes anyone with a basically happy marriage falling in love with another orgiast. The people who attend sex parties are there not because of romantic hungers but because their sexual drives need revitalization. New sexual partners give these people the sensual thrills and gratification they long for. Husbands and wives say orgies also have a salutory effect on day-to-day sex, as the excitement of an orgy carries over into regular lovemaking for several days or weeks afterward.

Although, using the above arguments, it

would seem that only married people would be interested in orgies, many single people attend swinging affairs. Since single people have more opportunity and freedom to choose as many sexual partners as they want and copulate with them any night of the week they choose, it's understandable that singles are usually outnumbered by marrieds at orgies, but the orgy scene is open to all who are interested. Marital status is unimportant in most groups.

Now you may have noticed that I'm not gushing over how wonderful I think orgies are and urging you to run right out and join the fun. That's because I think that swinging can present a major psychological problem for many women. If you throw your body open to all who want to grab for it, you run the danger of not respecting and valuing yourself highly enough, an attitude that will put you in a defensive situation in your relationships with the opposite sex. I can see the benefits, if you have been married for a long time, of attending an orgy once or twice a year, but to make it a regular part of your life would, in my opinion, take something away from your relationship with your husband. Sex with him can hardly seem as personal and important if you both have been in bed with four or five other people that week. Think it over carefully before you join a swinging group.

Of course, if you are single, you can juggle a hectic sex life and never let one man know about the other. An occasional or even regular foray into the world of orgies can be your secret.

If you are about to attend your first orgy, I have been given these pointers by several swingers to make your initial experience more comfortable for you:

1. Bring your own grapes—meaning, in this case, a man you know well and with whom you have a good sexual relationship. He must be already familiar with the orgy scene so that he can protect you tactfully from men whose advances you'd rather avoid. Your escort serves a second purpose, which is that, if you don't like *any* of the men you meet at the scene, you have brought a good sex partner with you.

2. Don't wear a dress that is fragile, as often there are not enough hangers and closets to put clothes in and that beaded chiffon of yours will probably have to be draped across a chair along with two or three other people's things.

3. If you are menstruating, stay home.

4. Do be prepared for the fact that you will be

expected to walk around naked.

5. And also realize that you will not have privacy. Anyone and everyone at the party is likely to barge in on you while you are copulating and anyone may even decide to join you and your partner.

6. There are sometimes lesbians at orgies who may make passes at you. If you realize this in advance, you should be able to handle the situation gracefully when it arises.

7. Expect to be nervous in the beginning. It might be wise to ask your escort to be your first lover of the evening. Since he is familiar to you, you won't be frightened. After you've broken the ice with him, then you will feel more relaxed with your unknown lovers.

8. Unless you live in Hollywood, don't expect the men to be glamorous movie star types. Most of the males are average in appearance and personality.

9. Because you are giving your body, don't expect to be treated like either a princess or a whore. At orgies, equality of the sexes is a reality.

10. If you are foolish enough to get pregnant from your peccadillo, no one is going to come to your aid financially or otherwise. Especially since any one of several men could be the father. Take adequate birth control precautions.

11. Oh. A last pointer. If it turns out that you *love* orgies, don't let guilt feelings spoil them for you. As an adult you have every right and responsibility to find a satisfactory sex life for yourself. If the orgy scene is your cup of tea, relax and enjoy it. Just don't righteously try to explain your new sexual philosophy and actions to your aging mother in Duluth. Let her rock away in the porch swing in peace.

17.

Where to Meet Men

There are some women who could drop a handkerchief in the middle of a deserted forest and suddenly there would be three men there to pick it up.

I, alas, have never been an instant male magnet and have always had to go where the men are to get my handkerchiefs retrieved.

But it's certainly worth the trip.

Unless you live at the North Pole or in the

middle of the Sahara Desert, it's easy enough to find hundreds of specimens of the opposite sex—just go out on the street or to a football game. You ll stumble over enough men to last Catherine the Great (and you) a lifetime.

But let's look at this practically. It's not enough to go to an area populated by men. You must also be able to sort out the impossibles quickly and get yourself in the company of men who are likely to interest you.

The *One Hundred Percent Impossibles* are easy to pick out: boys under the age of ten, the blatant homosexual (latent is something else again—that's harder) and the senile are good examples of complete time wasters.

The *Almost Impossibles* could be subtitled Stay Away Unless You Can Absorb a Great Deal of Pain, because they come with a big bag of troubles. These men include alcoholics, criminals, the insane, obsessive gamblers, sadists, masochists, dope pushers, drug addicts, pimps, Don Juans, the permanently bedridden, religious fanatics and men who refuse to work.

We *are* weeding them out, aren't we?

The next group are *men you couldn't like no matter what.* They may be *somebody's* adorables, but not yours. Perhaps they weigh three hundred and eighty pounds, smell and spit on the floor or they paw you every chance they get and scratch their genitals in public, are slimy, oily, evil or unbearably crude, stupid, dirty or sly, and you know instantly you can't stand them and no amount of exposure could change your mind.

With that charming group disposed of, you are now ready to focus on *The Possibles* and *The Probables.*

To be able to measure quickly the potential of a Possible takes experience—lots of dating and loving experience with different kinds of men so your radar can pick up the signals that will enable you to assess speedily the ones who aren't your type.

For instance, if your teeth start to chatter at the very word chill, let alone the actuality of a drafty room, and you meet a delightful man one January day at a party who says he never wears an overcoat, let that warning sign register, for he probably sleeps in a room with no heat and the windows open, even if it's ten degrees below zero outside. You'd have pneumonia within a week of taking up housekeeping with him—that is, after you recovered from that nasty head cold. Be nice, though, and pass him on to your friend who's such a winter sports nut.

164

One of the most beautiful love affairs of my life finally disintegrated under the pressure of our entirely different inner clocks. I am a night owl. The later it gets, the livelier I get. The minute the dawn begins to sneak through my window I turn to lead. Morning is an agony for me. I can't think, I can't move, I can't talk, my head aches and my stomach turns over at the sight or smell of food.

He, unfortunately, was the reverse. Along about ten in the evening, no matter how sparkling I was, he began to fade out. But, come five or six in the morning, he was prodding me awake with a steady stream of conversation about the world situation, what we were going to do that day, what did I think about this? What did I think about that? Then he would bounce joyfully out of bed and wait eagerly for me to fix that six-course breakfast, beginning with the freshly squeezed orange juice, four and one-half minute eggs, and so on.

The only way I was able to fix those breakfasts and talk to him in the morning was to stay up all night. Three months of practically no sleep and I collapsed. He, all concern and loving attention, insisted that from then on he would get up silently by himself and fix his own breakfast. It didn't work. He can't cook and he

165

was unhappy and lonely not sharing what was the best part of the day for him. We called our love affair off.

Ever since that experience, I have learned never to give my heart to an early-morning dynamo, and it takes me practically no time at all to spot one.

This does mean that you have to give up some real prizes. I passed on a handsome, sexy, bright and wealthy widower with three children to a neighbor of mine four years ago after just one date. Over dinner he had told me that every morning during the winter he and the children skied for an hour before breakfast. In summer they went for invigorating two-mile swims in the icy dawn. What he was looking for was a woman to marry who could share the beauty of this ritual. Even if I had been able to handle the time element, I'd have failed the athletic test. I can barely make it across the width of a junior wading pool without drowning. There was no question in my mind. I was not the lady for that gentleman.

There are many Possibilities that you can learn to discard quickly and save both of you time. If you enjoy only Mozart and Beethoven and he is the lead man in a rock and roll group, you are probably doomed as long-term lovers. I don't care if he does have hypnotic eyes and exudes sex, save your emotional energies for someone more promising.

If you are a gourmet cook and he insists on pouring half a bottle of ketchup on everything he eats, you are going to begin hating him every time you have to face him across the dining table. Send him on to your girl friend who cooks everything, including tomatoes, in ketchup.

There are some Possibles who are nice, do interesting work, have money in the bank, take well to children and married life, are attractive looking—have everything to recommend them really—but no matter how much you like them as *people,* as lovers they don't turn you on. My personal opinion on this is that if, after you give the man a real try, there's no chemistry between you, you should pass him on to your sister and/or turn him into a friend. Contrary to what is implied in some marriage manuals, I don't think you can manufacture that chemistry that makes life between the sexes worthwhile. You can make chemistry blossom, but you can't create it.

Efficiently weeding out the Possibles who

are impossible for *you* will still leave you with a sizable group of Possibles to develop plus the Tiffany group of *Probables*.

I believe in a double-pronged approach to reach these remaining men—General and Systematic.

The General Approach is to go to every party you are invited to, every political meeting, community event, concert or whatever that might also attract a Possibility. That includes jury duty. Since everyone has to serve, *he* might be there.

Don't discourage your friends from matchmaking. Even if the last three times around they have paired you with men who would make the most desperate spinster in your section of the country flee, the next one out of the box just might be a Prince.

That happened to me. My friends Ted and Marge, determined to marry me off, had dragged home three horrors for my inspection. The first one was a bookkeeper who didn't drink, smoke, go to movies or read books and who kept a house full of pet snakes. I still get a little queasy when I think of him. Number two was a used car salesman who called me "girlie" and pinched my bottom every time he

168

thought no one was looking, and number three was a writer (a pretty good writer at that) who hadn't brushed his teeth for at least ten years.

Number four, whom I had to be dragged to meet, kicking and screaming all the way, looked like John Kennedy, had the sensitivities of a poet, the sensuality of Richard Burton and a sense of humor besides. He was worth the time I had lost on the horrors.

Never let up on the General Approach, even if you are doing well with the Systematic, for the fates are peculiar and they're likely to plop down your Probable in the most unlikely place you could imagine.

The Systematic Approach is this. Sit down and decide exactly what kind of man attracts you and is *good* for you and then go about tracking him methodically.

Let me give you an example. Barbara had a glamour job as secretary to one of America's leading theatrical producers and access to some of the most fabled men in show business (they all came through her office eventually and many asked her out). Sound perfect? Not for Barbara. She realized one day that this plum of a job was a dead end for her because the kind of men who turned her on were not the flamboyant, emotional personalities common to show business. Instead, she was melted by quiet, solid, introverted engineer types.

When this realization hit Barbara, she got herself a list of all the engineering firms in New York City. A great number of them were located in the huge Engineering Building on East 47th Street, so she wrote letters of application to the Personnel Departments of three of the bigger companies in that building and shortly afterward took a job with one of those firms (the one that was growing the fastest and had the most young men in it). Before she knew it, Barbara was up to her ears in engineers. She couldn't avoid them. They were in every office, the halls, the elevators, the snack shop, everywhere she went.

That's the Systematic Approach.

Let me give you another example. When Vera got her divorce from her printing salesman husband, Ralph, she swore she would never go to another nightclub again. (He practically lived in nightclubs entertaining clients.) She wanted a rugged outdoor man, someone who could lift something heftier than a double martini.

Realizing that Chicago wasn't the ideal hunting grounds, she and the children moved to

170

Oregon (her cousin had a farm there just outside of Eugene) and found *him* almost immediately. He owned one of the farms adjoining her cousin's.

Vera hit pay dirt right away. She was inordinately lucky. But she said that, if the pickings in Eugene had been poor and she couldn't find the man she was dreaming of, she wouldn't have been discouraged at all—she would just have tried another area of the country. Maybe Wyoming or Missouri. For she knew he was out there and that it was only a matter of time (and using her head) before she found him.

Loretta had her heart set on a lawyer. She didn't have the skills or aptitude to become a legal secretary, but she joined the local Republican Club (lots of lawyers are politically minded) and did volunteer work. While she did meet lawyers, none was to her liking, so Loretta, being nonpartisan, switched over to the Democratic Club. There she started dating a Possible. When he didn't pan out, she turned to the Conservative Party and found a William Buckley type who met all her specifications. Her only problem now that they're married is that he spends too much of his leisure time on political activities. But that she should have figured.

171

My friend Karen is nutty about doctors, so she's doing volunteer hospital work. She hasn't met *the* doctor yet, but if she has to volunteer at every hospital in town she'll eventually track him down.

I have a weakness for men in the communications industries so I made friends and got jobs with people in the TV, radio and publishing fields. I was surrounded all day by men who attracted and stimulated me and met others at night through dinner parties and cocktail parties given by friends of mine who were also in those fields.

If I had a yen for the academic type, I wouldn't surround myself with electricians. If I wanted an oceanographer, I wouldn't look for him in Kansas.

Right?

Figure out what your dream man would probably do and get yourself as close as possible to his world.

So far in this chapter I have been primarily advising single women, widows and divorcees. If you are married, intend to stay married but yearn for a lover, you don't have quite the same mobility as the single woman. Especially if your husband won't allow you to work. If you have preschool-age children and limited funds for babysitters, it will be even harder. But not impossible. You still have access to a number of men whom you would never consider as husbands, but who would be more than adequate as lovers. The fact that a man is constantly overdrawn at the bank and unable to hold on to a dollar, or is chintzy about letting his wife have and use charge accounts, doesn't mean he wouldn't be a perfectly good part-time bed partner for you.

I am not personally pushing you to involve yourself in the intrigue of infidelity. Being a romantic, I hope you and your husband have such a great time in bed that you don't have any sexual energy left for another man. But not all people are married because they like each other. I'm not going to sit in moral judgment against you if you feel your personal circumstances would be improved by taking a lover. This section will tell you *how*, not *if*, you should cheat.

Who are your prospective lovers? They are men in your community who have the job mobility that enables them to meet you at odd hours of the day or night discreetly.

Where are these men? All around you. Take another look at your children's piano teacher. Or the piano tuner. Many of them are swinging ex-musicians. How about your golf pro or that muscular gentleman who gives you tennis lessons? Newspaper reporters have erratic schedules and often erotic natures. Portrait photographers are always popping in and out of homes without any questions being asked. Get out the phone book, make a list of photographers and go portrait shopping.

Almost all high schools have adult education courses. Take a night course in creative writing or woodworking or some such. You might find a soul mate who has no objections to cutting a few classes with you.

If you have a large, bare yard, get an estimate from that handsome landscape architect. He may give you a free hedge to conceal his love affair with you from your neighbor's prying eyes.

If you live in an academic community, grab yourself a professor. Scholarly types can always get away for hours at a stretch, if they find you attractive. Watch out for jealous female students though, who might write anonymous letters to your husband. It has happened before.

Some of the men you come in contact with are complete washouts. Insurance men only want to sell insurance. Fuller Brush men are too square. Dance instructors quite often like other men, not women. Plasterers and painters don't seem to have any urges stronger than the ones that drive them to make a complete mess of your house. Forget supermarket managers and shoe salesmen. By the end of the day they *hate* women.

In spite of the fact that they make house calls, doctors are usually wary of being seduced by patients. But if you are an urban dweller you might be able to snag your favorite specialist. Doctors in cities have more illicit affairs than doctors in the suburbs or country, because a suburban doctor is leery of parking his easily recognized car (those MD license plates, remember) in front of the same house too often when everyone on the block knows the occupant never had a sick day in her life. Doctors are nervous, too, about any hankypanky during office examinations for fear of getting slapped with a scandalous lawsuit. You're going to have to entice your medic out of his office if you want a *complete* physical.

There are all sorts of repairmen, deliverymen and delivery *boys*. I would especially recommend that you keep *away* from the grocery boy. Almost invariably he is a gossip and won't be able to resist bragging about what he's been delivering to *you*. There is a good possibility that he will boast of his exploits not only to his juvenile cohorts but to your worst enemy.

You may have good feelings about door-to-door magazine salesmen. I'm always convinced they're offering me a great price on the *Ladies' Home Journal* just to lull me into opening the door, whereupon they will pounce on me, slit my throat and steal my great-grandmother's diamond and garnet brooch.

I either buy my magazine subscriptions by telephone or go to my friendly neighborhood newsstand where the proprietor is one hundred and eight and has arthritis in both legs. I could outrun *him* with a year's supply of the Sunday edition of the *New York Times* piled on my back.

I am also afraid to pick up strange men on the street. With my luck I'd get Jack the Ripper or a plain-clothes policeman.

The *best* way for a married woman to meet prospective lovers is through her husband. He works all day with men, several of whom you'd probably adore. If you're absolutely determined to have no conscience, encourage your husband to introduce you to his business associates. Or give a party. His stockbroker, his lawyer, that V.P. in marketing he has lunch with once a week can be easily scanned during that big cocktail party you're giving next month if your husband can be induced to invite them. But no fair complaining if your husband starts chasing his stockbroker's wife. Remember those naughty, naughty intentions in *your* pretty little head.

All women—married, single, widowed or divorced—have trouble at one time or another in their lives finding men that please them. Even the most glamorous woman sometimes hits a dry spell. When it happens to you, don't get depressed. Experiment with a new hair styling, buy an extravagantly feminine dress on sale, go on a diet, redecorate your bedroom, do constructive female-type things that will keep your spirits up and be sure at this low time to double your man-hunting activity, using both the General and Systematic man-hunting approaches. It won't be long before you hit real gold again.

18.

Orgasm—Yours, Not His

Every now and then the Sensuous Woman finds it necessary to pull out of her bag of pleasures one of her top skills—The Sarah Bernhardt.

She acts.

Already I can hear you yowling *why*, if you are so adept at responding sexually, should you have to pretend?

How dare I, after spending seventeen chapters telling you to be sexy and real, now suddenly tell you to be fake!

I dare because I am practical.

No matter how sensual you are, there will be days when you don't feel like making love. You may have a cold, or be extremely tired from overwork and pressure or, somehow, no matter how you push it and will it, have trouble getting your body to come completely alive. That happens to all women, even sexy you.

But men's sexual drives don't always coincide with women's peaks. Quite often men are most ardent during female lows.

There are times when you can quite legitimately say, "I love you, but I can't make love right now," but no woman of any sensitivity would refuse to make love to a man she cares for, just because she "doesn't really feel like it." You focus like mad on all the fantasies that stir your sexual juices, concentrate on making your body respond to the highest point possible and, if you really can't get to orgasm, to avoid disappointing him and spoiling his plateau of excitement and sexiness, you fake that orgasm.

If you do it well, he won't be able to tell. Surprising, I know, but true.

179

I've never met a woman yet who didn't occasionally fake it.

And if you feel very Bernhardtish and want to throw in a few extra wriggles and a yelp or two along the way, to match his passion, go ahead. But be careful not to ham it up too much. Then he really will suspect you're acting and feel very disillusioned and inadequate, which is, of course, the opposite of the response you are lovingly trying to create.

Women have been faking since time began. Some of the biggest fakes have been women famous for their sexual prowess—courtesans, mistresses, love goddesses. When in some instances their lives or reputations depended upon their being a hot and erotic playmate, those ladies weren't about to let a little lack of true passion interfere with their lovemaking. They acted their beautiful little heads and bodies off. If a sex goddess gets up on the wrong side of the bed and her man wants to make love, she climbs right back into that bed and stays there until she has him climbing the headboard with ecstasy. She's not going to let the word get around that she's a poor bedmate.

If some of the really luscious women in the world feel that it's only good sense to fake it every now and then, give some thought to learning to be an expert fake yourself. There are three good reasons for it:

1. You make him happy.
2. A happy lover comes back again, and the next time you will probably be wild with passion and can hardly wait to make love.
3. Sometimes, if you are a really proficient actress, you fake yourself right into a *real* orgasm.

To become a fabulous fake, study again every contortion, muscle spasm and body response that lead to and make up the orgasm and rehearse the process privately until you can duplicate it.

But, keep very clearly in mind that, no matter how furious you become at him, no matter how much you may at some moment want to hurt him, no matter how much you may want to temporarily destroy him, you must *never, never* reveal to him that you have acted sometimes in bed.

You will betray a trust shared by every other female in the world if you do.

There are some secrets each sex should never reveal to the other. This is one of them.

And, on the practical side again, if you do squeal and later patch up the disagreement, you will have lost part of him, for he will never, ever fully trust or fully enjoy you in bed again.

That is a very heavy price to pay for a big mouth.

19.

Orgasm—His, Not Yours

I've never heard anything more ridiculous than the nonsense that has been perpetrated in recent years to the effect that the only way two people can reach authentic fulfillment together sexually is by having simultaneous orgasms.

This kind of propaganda is sad, for couples who believe it deprive themselves of one of the best parts of sex—feeling the partner coming to climax.

For a woman there is a special sweetness, tenderness, pride and, yes, even sense of power that she cheats herself of knowing if she is busy with her own orgasm while he is having his.

Here you've put in all this loving effort to excite and please him sexually. Aren't you entitled to be there for the culmination of your artistry? You can have a whole string of climaxes during intercourse, but he's probably only going to have one, so don't let any marriage manual talk you into missing that moment when he explodes in you. *Feel* the contractions of his penis and his whole body as he surrenders himself completely to the ecstasy of your body and pours his love into your loving vessel.

He will never be more yours than at that moment.

20.

Love, Love, Glorious Love

I've talked so much about tactile sensitivity, physical skills, sexual appetite and the importance of giving yourself to lovemaking with real enthusiasm—

I've warned you of woman's most deadly sexual enemy: familiarity—

I've made you aware of your greatest allies in sexually holding a man: imagination, perceiving his moods and desires and the courage to experiment with new techniques, enticing situations and places—

And I've pointed out how to pluck your dream man out of the field more efficiently—

But have I talked enough of *love?*

For it's love that makes a woman whole.

And gives her existence a sense of purpose.

Respect it, revel in it and learn to *understand* it.

You can enjoy yourself sexually without love and be physically satisfied, but only with love can you be *fulfilled.*

I recommend love highly.

It will cause you heartbreak only if you:

1. Use poor judgment in selecting the object of your affections.
2. Fail to grasp the entirely different role love plays in a man's existence.

Many women have needlessly suffered hurt, anxiety and anger because they have not understood that a man loves differently from a woman.

To a man, love and life are things apart.

To a woman, love is life itself.

By fully comprehending this, you will save yourself a lot of tears.

It is not unnatural for him to forget all about

186

you for hours at a time, even though he loves you dearly. But it is natural for you to be unable to erase him from your mind and body, no matter how hard you try.

Part of the reason for this is the kinds of activities that fill his days and yours. Yours almost all relate to him, his are completely divorced from you. When you shop for the groceries, you purchase with his food tastes in mind. When you do the laundry you handle his intimate clothing—underwear, socks, etc.—and automatically think of him. As you try on a new dress you wonder, "Will he think it is pretty?" When you overload the charge accounts or ruin his favorite knife by using it to pry open a sticky cabinet door, you are nervous over his possible anger.

But none of his activities during the day are likely to remind him of you. There is nothing in the thirty-page report he's preparing on fiscal trends in the ball-bearing industry that will make his thoughts stray to you. He is not going to brood about your possible reaction when he calls a meeting of his department to plan the new promotion on heavy-duty tractors. You may worry about how his appointment went with Consolidated Sales this morning, but he will never give a thought to whether you were

187

able to clean the children's room or give that luncheon without a hitch. The one time when he is likely to think of you is when he is looking at a luncheon menu. He will try to guess what you are planning for dinner so he won't have lamb chops or beef stew twice in the same day.

Aside from the difference in his daily activities, there is another psychological aspect to his work that precludes his sitting around in a sentimental haze over you. And that is that most men are as wedded to and as passionate about their careers as they are about women. I'm afraid it is the nature of the male, so relax and accept the reality and the permanence of the situation.

Since he is unable to love you one hundred percent of the time, should you retaliate in kind?

Absolutely not! You would be insane to go against your nature and cheat yourself of many tender, sweet, entirely female moments such as daydreaming of his wondrous qualities and endearing ways; or the building excitement that leads to his homecoming every day, or the many thoughtful little things you do lovingly to make his life more comfortable that give you so much satisfaction.

188

LOVE, LOVE, GLORIOUS LOVE

We women were born to love, and only when we love to capacity are we happy.

So—love, love, glorious love.

Don't be afraid of it.

Do let love into every aspect of your life.

21.

Contentment . . .

Well, here we are at the end. I'm never going to write another book even if I find a method of having fifty orgasms in one minute flat.

Being typically female, I have saved one of the most important statements for last, and I'm going to have a lot of people nipping at me if I don't make this clear: I am not a psychiatrist, psychologist, gynecologist, trained researcher or any other kind of expert. I haven't even mastered the revolving door or the electric can opener yet, let alone the stacks of technical papers on human sexuality.

This is definitely an "unofficial" book by a laywoman (if you'll excuse the pun).

An unbelievably happy laywoman, for as I lie here (I probably shouldn't admit it, but I write in bed) putting the finishing touches on *The Sensuous Woman*, next to me is the man I have always dreamed of but up until five years ago never stood a chance of getting.

I won his love by becoming a Sensuous Woman and that's how I keep him coming eagerly home to me each night.

To get him I did just about everything in this book. I know my method works even when the odds are stacked the other way, because you should have seen my competition! One lady looked like Grace Kelly and the other was the equal of Sophia Loren.

Now I, on my best day, wouldn't be able to hold a mascara brush to those two ladies, who were also intelligent, charming and clever.

Yet he left those two gorgeous creatures for *me*. Believe me, it was no accident. A miracle, maybe, but an accident, no.

I've gone ahead and built myself a truly beautiful sexual and romantic life, and you, I believe with all my heart, will experience the same miracle of love and fulfillment if you follow the method in this book.

Come on now. Get moving. You're going to have a wonderful time! Just think of all that sexual happiness and those delicious men who are coming your way.

You are going to adore being a Sensuous Woman.

Now if you'll excuse me, I'm just going to turn over and, starting with the Silken Swirl and the Butterfly Flick, drive my man, and *me*, to ecstasy.

UHMMMMMM

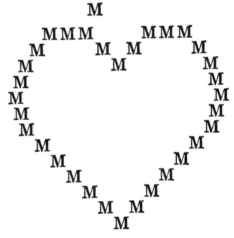